STRATFORD PAPERS
1965–67

STRATFORD PAPERS
1965–67

edited by B. A. W. Jackson

McMaster University Library Press

Irish University Press

© McMaster University Library Press,
Canada, 1969

SBN 7165 0522 3

Irish University Press Shannon Ireland

DUBLIN   CORK   BELFAST   LONDON   NEW YORK

Captain T M MacGlinchey Publisher

PRINTED IN THE REPUBLIC OF IRELAND AT SHANNON
BY ROBERT HOGG PRINTER TO IRISH UNIVERSITY PRESS

CONTENTS

v

PREFACE

Since 1960, Shakespeare Seminars have been held annually at Stratford, Ontario. These Seminars have been sponsored and organized by McMaster University and conducted with the co-operation of the Stratford Festival. Each Seminar brings together about a hundred and fifty assorted Shakespeare enthusiasts, and combines a week of theatre-going with formal and informal discussions of the season's plays and productions, tours of the Festival Theatre and talks by scholars, critics, actors, directors and others intimately involved with the Theatre or with Shakespeare's works. Although some specialists attend, the Seminars are not designed for specialists only, but for all those for whom Shakespeare and theatre are requirements of the good life.

This volume is a collection of some of the papers delivered at the Seminars held in the summers of 1965–67. We should explain that for five years from the beginning of the Seminars in 1960, we published each year's papers in an annual volume, but a combination of circumstances forced us to abandon regular publication following the volume for 1964. In 1965 we published a few of the summer's papers in what we referred to at the time as a 'stop-gap edition' made possible by the courtesy of the Printing Department of the University. In the preface to that volume I wrote hopefully: 'Following the 1966 Seminars, we plan to bring out our regular volume again, and to publish in it not only the 1966 lectures but those of 1965 as well, including the ones already printed here. In this way the series will remain intact, except that two years' Seminars will be contained in one book.'

Vain hope, and unfulfilled promise! It is only now that we are in a position to resume publication with a collection of papers from three summers' Seminars. The next volume, planned for 1969, will include more papers from these years, and others from 1968 and 1969; we hope that other volumes will follow in future years.

We regret that a number of people with sufficient faith in our publication to place standing orders for the annual volumes have been disappointed over the past three years. We apologize for their inconvenience and hope we may continue to enjoy their support. We are grateful for their interest and inquiries, which have encouraged our belief that papers presented originally to an audience united by their love for Shakespeare will find readers among the numberless company who share their feelings.

We regret too that some readers present at the Seminars during which these papers were delivered will mourn the absence of other papers given at the same sessions. A number of these have been published elsewhere; others, deliberately designed only for oral presentation, can live only in the memories of those who enjoyed hearing them. The papers printed here keep the qualities of lectures, and documentation has been kept to a minimum.

We wish to thank our contributors for making this volume possible, and all our speakers and discussion leaders, along with the staff of the Festival Theatre, for making possible the Seminars at which these papers are first delivered. We are indebted to Professor W. B. Ready, McMaster's Librarian, for his assistance in arranging for the *Stratford Papers* to resume publication, and to the Canada Council and the University for their support of the Seminars.

McMaster University   B. W. Jackson
October 1968

THE TEACHING OF SHAKESPEARE

L. C. Knights

Of all the tributes to Shakespeare that appeared in the quatercentenary year the one I most enjoyed was the article by James Baldwin on 'Why I Stopped Hating Shakespeare' that appeared in the London *Observer* (19 April 1964). In it Baldwin told of his early incomprehension and dislike—a dislike amounting to hatred for a powerful, inescapable but alien force—and of the way his feelings suddenly changed:

> I still remember my shock [he wrote] when I finally *heard* these lines from the murder scene in Julius Caesar. The assassins are washing their hands in Caesar's blood. Cassius says:
>
> > Stoop then, and wash. —How many ages hence
> > Shall this our lofty scene be acted over,
> > In states unborn and accents yet unknown!
>
> What I suddenly heard, for the first time, was manifold. It was the voice of lonely, dedicated, deluded Cassius, whose life had never been real for me before—I suddenly seemed to know what this moment meant to him. But beneath and beyond that voice I also heard a note yet more rigorous and impersonal—and contemporary: that 'lofty scene', in all its blood and necessary folly, its blind and necessary pain, was thrown into a perspective which has never left my mind. Just so, indeed, is the heedless State overthrown by men, who, in order to overthrow it, have had to achieve a desparate single-mindedness. And this single-mindedness which we think of (why?) as ennobling, also operates, and much more surely, to distort and diminish a man—to distort

I

and diminish us all, even, or perhaps especially, those whose needs and whose energy made the overthrow of the State inevitable, necessary and just.

From that moment, Baldwin says, his quarrel with the English language because it did not reflect his own experience was transformed into the recognition of a challenge. This language, which could so powerfully transmit experience, could perhaps be used to express his own experience: there could be, so to speak, a two-way commerce:

> My relationship, then, to the language of Shakespeare revealed itself as nothing less than my relationship to myself and my past. Under this light, this revelation, both myself and my past began slowly to open, perhaps the way a flower opens at morning, but, more probably, the way an atrophied muscle begins to function, or frozen fingers to thaw.

Since Baldwin is an American negro and a novelist, there were complications in his relationship to Shakespeare that do not concern us here. I quote from his article because it seems to me to describe in a completely authentic way the *kind* of personal awakening that we should like to be able to hope for for each of our pupils, sooner or later, in their reading of Shakespeare.

Not long ago I had dinner with a group of medical students who had just taken their final examination. As the conversation eased my neighbours turned to me with a question that was obviously more than dinner-table chat. 'Here we are', they said, 'at the end of our professional education, and we feel completely uneducated in things that are important to us as human beings. What should we read? How do we get to know literature in a way that really matters to us? We have been streamed as scientists ever since the fifth form, and there is a world of experience that we know virtually nothing of. Can't you tell us where to make a start?' This question,

2

from a group of obviously intelligent young men, jerked me out of all the assumptions I habitually make as a professor of English. Here was something real, and its effect was to make the world of English scholarship, English teaching and literary criticism seem enclosed and inadequate. And this sense of people putting out their hands for something they desperately need and not getting it, is what we must all sometimes feel when we consider not only the education of scientists, but education in its widest range. Those of us who teach Shakespeare, teach literature, are really in a very strange situation. On the one hand there is all the apparatus of scholarship and formal education—the Shakespeare industry, the multiplication of specialist studies, Shakespeare as an examination subject; on the other hand there is the fact that many people who are quite capable of reading and responding to Shakespeare in a personal way either don't read him at all, or regard him as part of a 'culture' that has no very direct contact with their own lives.

There is no need to make the picture too black. Shakespearian scholarship has its uses; the plays set for examination are often better edited than they used to be, and they always offer an opportunity in the classroom; and Shakespeare *can* come alive at school—as one sees from time to time in good school productions. But the fact remains that very many people—people who need the rich humanizing experience of great literature, and Shakespeare above all—experience James Baldwin's unawareness without the awakening—the thawing of frozen fingers—that he describes so well.

We can't, really, come to grips with this situation without raising the general question: Why do we teach literature? To which the short answer is, so that as many people as possible shall share the imaginative life that is 'stored' in the great masterpieces, so that their own imaginative-creative life may

3

be quickened. Obviously what is in question is not 'knowing about' the masterpieces, but a genuine response from a personal centre—the only way in which great literature can become part of our own lives. That is easy to say: the difficult thing is to make it a reality. How do we achieve an aim that is so important and yet so difficult to define, because the result (if we call it that) will be something different for each individual pupil, and probably something different from anything we could have foreseen? To the question I have just asked there is no answer that can be offered ready-made. As teachers we each have to find our own way over a considerable period of time. I can only offer some thoughts of my own on the teaching of Shakespeare, with the kind of aim I have indicated. And before I try to put those thoughts in order let me offer one more caution: remember that you can't *make* people see; you can only provide opportunities and—in the way you present material that is so much more important than anything that can be said about it—prompt them to do their own seeing.

Art enhances the sense of being alive. Imagination is a form of energy. The Shakespearian energy—the vitality that is at one and the same time strength and firmness and the most delicate awareness of shades of feeling and thought—is what I really want to talk about—that, and the way it can communicate itself, can call out something corresponding in reader or spectator. It is an energy that shows itself in the overall design of each play, and in the minutest details of which each play is composed. For reasons that will appear in a moment, I do not want to say that the enjoyment and understanding of Shakespeare begins with the conscious enjoyment of his poetic energy, and that therefore the foundation of our teaching is to call attention to the marvellous and infinitely varied ways in which his poetry works.

Yet clearly unless there is some sense that everything depends on the imaginative 'charge' of the language, that action and character, theme and structure—all the things that I am going to talk about before long—simply would not exist except in the precise words through which Shakespeare embodies them, then one is not really reading Shakespeare at all. And unless that sense accompanies our teaching, so that sometimes it flashes across between teacher and pupil, then we might as well set the class to reading textbook summaries of the plots of the plays.

I should like to pause here and dip a thimble in the ocean. The capacity for delight in words and what words can do varies, it seems, between person and person. But in some measure, unless inhibited by some emotional blockage, it is present in all young humans like a natural appetite. In this respect Shakespeare offers more than enough for appetite to feed on. It is not a very long step from enjoyment of the sheer vigour of expression in scorn or hatred—where it is enough to get the lines read aloud with some bodily weight behind them—

> All the infections that the sun sucks up
> From bogs, fens, flats, on Prosper fall. . . .
>
> You common cry of curs! whose breath I hate
> As reek o' the rotten fens. . . .
>
> A milk-sop, one that never in his life
> Felt so much cold as over shoes in snow

—it is not a very long step from that to enjoyment of different and subtler forms of expressive phrase. What we do learn of Tybalt's way of walking from Mercutio's taunt, 'Good king of cats'? What do we learn of Othello from the *tone* of the famous line, 'Keep up your bright swords, for the dew will rust them'?

Appreciation of poetry is of course much more than the savouring of individual lines and phrases. It depends above all on an ability, consciously or unconsciously, to make connections. Poetry, as Coleridge saw, is a power that brings things into unity. You remember the account given by one of the Tribunes in *Cariolanus* of the triumphant return of Caius Marcius to Rome:

> All tongues speak of him, and the bleared sights
> Are spectacled to see him: your prattling nurse
> Into a rapture lets her baby cry
> While she chats him: the kitchen malkin pins
> Her richest lockram 'bout her reechy neck
> Clambering the walls to eye him: stalls, bulks, windows,
> Are smother'd up, leads fill'd, and ridges hors'd
> With variable complexions, all agreeing
> In earnestness to see him.

I suppose the vigour of that is obvious at a first reading. It is also obvious that the effect is not only a matter of telling detail. The description, moving from a general impression of the crowd to vividly perceived particulars, and back again to a more general impression, is held together at the focus of all this excited interest: 'see him', 'chats him', 'eye him', 'see him'. It isn't only a description of a bustling crowd of people: just as the crowd is united in the common purpose of seeing or talking about the returning hero, so the passage is held together by the felt presence of Coriolanus, which is here mediated to us through the hostility and reluctant admiration of the Tribune. The passage enforces another point too that is important for our general discussion. The whole scene is in movement for us because Shakespeare makes us imagine so many people doing things—trivial things, but all indicative of haste and eagerness: old men are in the act of putting on their spectacles; a neglected baby is crying itself into a fit whilst the nurse eagerly gossips about the popular hero—'*chats him*', an unpoetical but vigorous phrase; the kitchen maid is still pinning on a bit of finery whilst she scuttles out to get a good view—'clambering the walls to eye him'; not only is every available vantage point 'smother'd' with the press of people, the roof-ridges are 'hors'd', as though those who had got there were riding them. It is as though the bustling activity of the crowd were communicated to our own minds as we read. But of course the truth is that we sense the movement of the crowd because our own minds are active—set in movement, as it were, by the vigour of Shakespeare's poetry.

Now of course the teacher need not *tell* his pupils much, if anything, about that activity. But it is his job to create conditions in which that activity can take place. The most favourable condition is a state of enjoyment, of active enlisted interest. Given that, very little explicit prompting is necessary for most people to see that making connections— allowing words and phrases to reach out to the context that modifies them, and that they in turn modify, 'the complete consort dancing together' in a living whole—that making connections is of the essence of understanding Shakespeare. In Macbeth's great despairing soliloquy, 'To-morrow, and to-morrow, and to-morrow', it is a small jump from 'the last syllable of recorded time' to 'life is *a tale* told by an idiot'; it is a bigger jump from 'make thick my blood, Stop up th'access and passage to Remorse' to 'Light thickens, And the crow makes wing to th'Rooky wood'; both jumps, or, better, both tentative reachings out, and many others, have to be made if *Macbeth* is to grow in our minds.

I suppose everyone here takes all this, or something like it, for granted, and there is no need for me to insist on the virtues of attentive reading. What I should like to do here briefly is to warn. You don't want to make Shakespeare, or any other great writer, simply an opportunity for 'doing Practical Criticism', What is commonly called 'close reading' is of course necessary—at all events with pupils of some maturity and experience of ranging reading. You don't get anything from pictures, music or poems unless you actively attend; and there will always be some among your pupils whose verbal sense is acute and capable of being very highly developed. But we have to remember also that there is such a thing as intuitive awareness, and that it can be inhibited by too great an insistence on verbal analysis. Over-insistence, insistence of the wrong kind, makes people strain to see: whereas our deepest awareness of all literature (as of music and the other arts) is paradoxically compounded: on the one hand there is the active, inquiring, building up of meanings; on the other there is deep, relaxed receptivity— and for many people the second is more important than the first. It is all a matter of tact on the part of the teacher, of not forcing what should be a natural growth. For my own part I think that in most teaching of Shakespeare explicit prompting to see what the words may be doing, here and here, should be done almost incidentally and as occasion offers. You don't want people who can talk about the structure of imagery in *Macbeth* without ever having experienced, really experienced, the play.

All the same, I can't imagine any teaching of Shakespeare that doesn't somehow suggest the power of Shakespeare's poetry. For what is growing as the poetry exerts its power is at the foundation of all enjoyment and all understanding of the plays. Let me repeat it once more. The characteristic of the poetry is energy; it is a unifying energy, and it reveals itself, communicates itself, as *we* make the connections through which the meaning is to be found. Putting this another way: the energy released in us, the active direction of mind and feeling as we make connections, *is* the meaning.

I have spent almost half my time on what are really preliminary matters—though I think matters of some importance. Let me turn now to more directly practical questions involved in the teaching of Shakespeare. We are concerned not only with life here and here in the poetry but with individual plays, each a world of experience into which we should like our pupils to enter. The practical question is, where do we start? Here again, and very obviously, there is no one answer. But there are various things we can keep in mind: things to which we can usefully direct our pupils, getting them to pause, to focus and deepen attention, to draw out significance and—above all—to connect. If I now list three or four possible 'ways in' to a deeper understanding it is not because I want to suggest a method, because there is no method; still less is it because I regard my list as exhaustive, for it clearly isn't; it is simply by way of producing examples of the kind of thing we each try to do in our different ways.

The first two 'ways in' take their start from interests that must surely be spontaneous and natural to every reader and spectator, for they concern respectively moments of high dramatic tension, and moments when what is immediately within and behind the lines—a speaker's 'character'—reveals itself with special fullness and force. In every reading of a play there are passages, often quite short, where the attention of even the most scatter-brained is gripped and held. It is of course theatrical effectiveness in the most obvious sense that grips the auditors. But since we are dealing with Shakespeare, the moments of great theatrical effectiveness are passages of condensed significance, where meanings flow together, so that to enter deeply into the significance of the moment is to find revealed something of the structure of meanings that constitute the play as a whole. It is, I think, the teacher's business, from time to time (and always with the tact that does not crassly interfere with what is going on in the pupil) to allow that sense of concentrated significance to unfold. The scene where Caesar's murderers stoop to wash their hands in Caesar's blood is one such scene, as James Baldwin found. Or consider the curt exchange between Macbeth and his wife as he comes from Duncan's room after killing the king:

MACBETH: I have done the deed—Didst thou not
                                      hear a noise?

LADY MACBETH: I heard the owl scream, and the crickets cry.
                  Did not you speak?

MACBETH: When?

LADY MACBETH: Now.

MACBETH: As I descended?

LADY MACBETH: Ay.

That is silence made palpable, in which the mere chirping of the crickets becomes a disturbing 'cry', and it continues to enwrap the speakers as Macbeth goes on to tell of the voice that cried, 'Sleep no more!'

    Glamis hath murther'd Sleep, and therefore Cawdor
    Shall sleep no more, Macbeth shall sleep no more!

And this uncanny, out-of-the-world atmosphere—what De Quincey called an 'awful parenthesis' between life's normal goings-on—continues until it is both broken and emphasized by the famous knocking at the gate of the castle. 'Wake Duncan with thy knocking,' says Macbeth, 'I would thou couldst!' All this is obviously good 'theatre'; but it is very much more than just that. For what it says, in terms that speak directly to our senses, is that at the moment of the murder Macbeth and his wife are isolated in a world of their own. Now this sense of the increasing isolation of the protagonists is part of the main imaginative impression of the play as a whole: when Macbeth plunges further into crime we are told that he 'keeps alone', he has no friends, his kingdom is a desert, his soldiers fly from him; at the end he cannot even mourn his wife's death—'She should have died hereafter.' This is, at least in part, an explanation of what I have called the uncanny atmosphere surrounding Macbeth and his wife at the moment of the murder of Duncan. For what the play insists on, as it proceeds, is that Macbeth's isolation is more than the necessary friendlessness of a tyrant, that more than social sanctions are involved: it is seen as resulting from a denial and violation of life, not only in his victims but in himself, in his own essential manhood. I do not say that the teacher should tell the class all this. I do say that if, without interfering or imposing, he can elicit something like this line of reflection *in terms of the play itself,* he will have done a service to his pupils: he will have let them see for themselves that there is a way in to the heart of the play from scenes that 'find' them without any prompting.

I suppose an interest in character, in the variety of human types and the way they express themselves, is as innate as the capacity to be absorbed in an exciting dramatic action. And here, as we all know, is one of the most obvious of the ways in to total dramatic significance. I do not want here to be bogged down in the debate—which is becoming tedious—of the meaning of the word 'character' in Shakespearian criticism.[1] It is enough to say here that what I mean is an attitude to life embodied with different degrees of fullness and explicitness, an 'address to the world' (in Arthur Sewell's useful phrase) that we find consistent and convincing. I suppose that in teaching Shakespeare there comes a stage

1 See 'The Question of Character in Shakespeare' in my *Further Explorations* (London 1964).

when we have to point out that to speak of the 'character' of the dramatis personae is sometimes more misleading than helpful; but with this proviso there is no reason why we should not enlist a naive pleasure in the representation of character for the part it can play in individual exploration and discovery—on two conditions. One is that attention should always be guided towards the words—the tone and idiom and general manner—in which a character announces itself. The other is that interest, once aroused, should be guided towards a recognition that the appreciation of vivid and impressive characters is not an end in itself, but that it takes its part in the recognition of a wider pattern: a pattern of relations of character to character, and of character to something wider and more inclusive—that overarching 'attitude to life' which *is* the play, though we can never reduce it to bare statement. In almost all Shakespeare's plays characters that are going to have an important part in the action announce themselves early through a particular way of speech that is felt with a sense of bodily presence. There is Volumnia's bluntly overbearing and insensitive, 'I pray you, daughter, sing; or express yourself in a more comfortable sort.' There is Othello's straightening of the shoulders in a subordinate clause as he disclaims the need for boasting:

> 'Tis yet to know—
> Which, when I know that boasting is an honour,
> I shall promulgate—I fetch my life and being
> From men of royal seige . . .

There is Macbeth's quick, nervous phrasing, and Hamlet's brooding, often repetitive, form of speech. Only a minimum of prompting is necessary to bring out something of what lies behind these characteristic rhythms and turns of phrase. It is a matter of getting people to recognize particular voices, and then to see something of their relation to each other. 'I weep for joy,' says Richard II on his return from Ireland to confront Bolingbroke,

> I weep for joy
> To stand upon my kingdom once again.
> Dear earth, I do salute thee with my hand,
> Though rebels wound thee with their horses' hoofs.
> As a long-parted mother with her child
> Plays fondly with her tears and smiles in meeting,
> So weeping, smiling, greet I thee, my earth,
> And do thee favours with my royal hands. . . .

If we are reading *Richard II* with a class, that is a voice they will, by now, have come to recognize—the dramatization, self-reference, the easy slide from reality. The whole speech and what immediately follows can indeed open up the whole play for us. For not only does the obvious self-indulgence in the passage I have quoted throw light on the subsequent claim to divine right, Richard's voice (and all that the voice conveys) is heard against the taciturnity (except when he is engaged in public rhetoric) of Bolingbroke. That contrast of course determines one of the main structural lines of the play; and when the two men are confronted—as at Flint Castle or in the deposition scene—or contrasted in parallel scenes, what necessarily comes into view is the contrast between two radically opposed political attitudes: not attitudes abstractly conceived (divine right versus Machiavellian 'realism') but as embodied. The political clash is seen in terms of the actual complexity of life (how do you weigh up the rights and wrongs of either side?), and public attitudes are revealed as rooted in the recesses of personality. A play rich in 'human interest' reveals itself as political fable, in and through which an uncommon wisdom can speak even to the unlearned.

What I am trying to say is that any genuine spontaneous interest, pursued with attention and enjoyment, can lead towards the imaginative centre of a Shakespearian play where each one must make his discoveries for himself. I think that marked dramatic tension and the revelation, in some sense, of character, are likely to hold the interest of young readers in a quite spontaneous way, and are therefore natural points of entry into the plays. There are of course others; though to the extent that they appeal to a slightly more mature interest and may therefore first spring up as a result of the teacher's prompting, there is a corresponding danger to be guarded against: I mean the danger of imposing an opinion that the pupil may only too easily mistake for his own reading of the play. If the prompting takes the form of questions, however, of a tentative and ready-to-withdraw probing to find what the pupil may be ready to see with his own eyes, then there seems no reason why these approaches should not be used with the rest. When King Lear says,

> Tremble, thou wretch,
> That hast within thee undivulged crimes,
> Unwhipped of justice,

what does this reveal not only of Lear's 'character' but, more especially, of his conception of justice? On the evidence of the play does Shakespeare endorse that conception? What about the denunciation of the beadle lashing the prostitute? How does the description of the mad beggar, 'whipp'd from tithing to tithing, and stock-punished, and imprisoned', fit into the whole picture? What about the mad mock-trial, where Lear attempts to 'have the law on' Goneril and Regan? How is all this related to Lear's initial attempt to apportion reward to what he conceives as merit—a sort of distributive justice? And, when he is reconciled to Cordelia, does he get exactly what he 'deserves'? These, no one can deny, raise questions that are of great importance within the play as a whole; and I suppose that for an adult reader the 'themes', or organizing interests that shape the whole dramatic structure of the greater plays, are a major part of what he feels the plays to be 'about'. In the classroom, even in the sixth form, such matters must, I think, be handled with caution because of the danger of abstraction. We can ask questions, we can hope that interests will be aroused that will develop in later life; but what we want in the first place is that our pupils shall have a life-enhancing experience, not that they harness and tame it with critical schemata.

There is, however, one further interest that, if not native to the untutored mind, very quickly takes root once it is planted: I mean an interest in form and structure, in the way the thing is made. Shakespeare, from the start, was a conscious and deliberate craftsman, and if the life of the plays is in a poetry more subtle and far-reaching than any other in the English language, the poetry speaks to us within, and as part of, a carefully contrived design. There are no recondite mysteries here; there is only a supreme skill in presentation that directs us towards the heart of the matter. I think for example of such apparently simple things as the sequence and juxtaposition of scenes. What is the effect of the alternation of main plot and subplot in *Henry IV*? of the alternation of events on the Heath and within Gloucester's castle in the third act of *King Lear*? Why almost immediately after we have seen Caius Marcius denouncing the plebs at the start of *Coriolanus* are we given a domestic scene in which his mother expounds her philosophy of life?[2] These are obvious, necessary and important questions. Simply by putting two and two together, as Shakespeare clearly if implicitly asks us to do, we are guided towards those matters that the play is expressly designed to present. All this is material for a long discussion, not for the almost concluding passage of a talk

2 Incidentally, why in *Henry V* are we given two different accounts of the battle of Crécy, and in *Julius Caesar* two different accounts, one in prospect and one in retrospect, of the murder of Caesar?

such as this. I can only point to two examples—one simple, the other more difficult—of the kind of thing I have in mind, and towards which our classroom teaching can be directed. The first act of *Richard II* is composed of four scenes. The first scene belongs to the public world, full of high-sounding rhetoric in which it is quite impossible to get at the truth that underlies the quarrel of the two lords. The second scene is a private scene: things are said (about the murder of the Duke of Gloucester) that cannot be said in public. The third scene is again one of show and spectacle and public posture, though by now we have some decidedly uneasy feelings about the king who ostensibly controls the proceedings. The fourth scene is private once more—Richard 'letting himself go' with his confidential advisers and personal friends —and it is a very unpleasant spectacle indeed. What is Shakespeare saying to us by means of this particular sequence, if not that public events are inescapably related to the private selves of those who determine those events, and that political wisdom consists in recognizing complex human realities that cannot possibly be summed up in the necessary sim-plifications of politics. And there is more too. This first act puts two men—two different political types—in sharp opposition. The play as a whole will develop that opposition, steadily deepening our sense of the radical ambiguity of political life. The last act, with its alternation of public scenes, and of scenes showing what goes on behind the public facade, virtually repeats the pattern of the first act, but now with Bolingbroke in the place of Richard. It seems deliberate and important: what it means is left to us to discover.

The discovery of formal principle in works so carefully constructed as Shakespeare's plays is of course so very much more than just that. If attention to simple contrast, juxta-position and variation *directs* our attention to crucial areas of experience to be explored, there is a sense in which something that can only be callèd formal structure is inseparable from meaning. Let me, as I draw towards an end, call your attention to two passages of rather striking poetry in *The Winter's Tale*. The first is when Leontes begins to give way to the distorted and distorting passion of jealousy:

> Thou want'st a rough pash, and the shoots that I have
> To be full, like me: yet they say we are
> Almost as like as eggs; women say so,
> (That will say anything). But were they false
> As o'er-dyed blacks, as wind, as waters: false
> As dice are to be wish'd, by one that fixes
> No bourn 'twixt his and mine; yet were it true,
> To say this boy were like me. Come (Sir Page)
> Look on me with your welkin eye: sweet villain,
> Most dear'st, my collop: Can thy dam, may't be
> Affection? thy intention stabs the centre.
> Thou dost make possible things not so held,
> Communicatest with Dreams (how can this be?)
> With what's unreal: thou coactive art,
> And fellow'st nothing. Then 'tis very credent,
> Thou mayest co-join with something, and thou dost,
> (And that beyond commission) and I find it,
> (And that to the infection of my brains,
> And hardening of my brows.)

The second forms part of the wooing of Perdita by Florizel in the great pastoral scene:

> What you do,
> Still betters what is done. When you speak (Sweet)
> I'ld have you do it ever: when you sing,
> I'ld have you buy, and sell so: so give alms,
> Pray so: and for the ordering your affairs,
> To sing them too. When you do dance, I wish you
> A wave o'the sea, that you might ever do
> Nothing but that: move still, still so:
> And own no other function. Each your doing,
> (So singular in each particular)
> Crowns what you are doing, in the present deeds,
> That all your acts, are queens.

The first of these speeches is, so to speak, a pivotal point in the first movement of the play, the next a significant and integral part of the second movement. The contrast is indeed obvious. Leontes' speech cannot be subsumed in any sort of rational order; there is an appearance of logic, but without the reality; and the pounce of the mind with which Leontes 'proves' his point is a gross commitment to illusion. Not only is the rhythm disturbed and broken ('he cracks his gorge, his sides, with violent hefts'), the dizzy vortex of feeling circles on the emphatic first personal pronoun. The speech is a perfect image of disintegration and self-enclosure. Florizel's speech is in every way a contrast. The diction is utterly simple, returning with varied insistence to the little common words 'do' and 'so'. There is a marked patterning of clause and phrase, but with such variation and rhythmical life that the pattern seems to be in movement: even before we come to the word 'dance' we know that it is something analogous to a dance that we are responding to. The speaker's attention is wholly held by something outside himself—the loved object—and yet in this entirely personal and lover-like celebration of Perdita's qualities there is a recognition of something beyond the merely personal; for the image of the wave of the sea, reinforced as it is by the extraordinary rhythm of the lines ('move still, still so') hints at a more-than-personal power behind the grace of the imagined dancer. Leontes' heart had 'danced' but in a different way—'my heart dances, But not for joy, not joy.' That contrast is, I think, what *The Winter's Tale* is about: that the relation of each of these opposed states to the fundamental drives of our nature, and the possibility of the first being somehow touched and transmuted by the grace of the second. Once more we find that Shakespeare guides our minds and sympathies—our imaginations—by asking us to attend, to contrast and actively to make connections.

I do not wish, in concluding, to attempt any formal summary of what I have said, for I hope the main points are clear. There are many ways into the experience of a Shakespeare play. Any way is the right way provided that it starts from a genuine personal engagement, and provided that an interest, once aroused, submits to the discipline of what is actually there before it—something that can lead it on to make further and further connections. How that process develops, in each different individual, must remain something of a mystery, and although the teacher can help, he must always remain aware of the limits of what he can do: he must always leave an area of privacy in which growth can take place. Martin Buber puts the matter well:

> . . . if the educator of our day has to act consciously he must nevertheless do it 'as though he did it not'. That raising of the finger, that questioning glance, are his genuine doing. Through him the selection of the effective world reaches the pupil. He fails the recipient when he presents this selection to him with a gesture of interference. It must be concentrated in him; and doing out of concentration has the appearance of rest. Interference divides the soul in his care into an obedient part and a rebellious part. But a hidden influence proceeding from his integrity has an integrating force.[3]

In the teaching of Shakespeare, as in all our teaching, much that we do not say—what we are and what we stand for, and how at the centre of ourselves we genuinely feel towards the work in hand—may have as much force as what we actually say, perhaps more. It is the teacher's attitude, expressed in questioning and non-dogmatic prompting, that can help the pupil to see the essential thing: that Shakespeare offers him opportunities of becoming more fully alive. It was Coleridge who said of Shakespeare, 'You feel him to be

3 Martin Buber, 'Education', *Between Man and Man,* p. 90.

a poet, inasmuch as for a time he has made you one—an active creative being.' To foster that sense—the sense of personal creative discovery—is the aim of our teaching, however far it may seem from the actualities of the classroom and the more obvious demands of the educational system.

August 1966

MANNER AND MEANING IN SHAKESPEARE'S PLAYS

Arthur Colby Sprague

Sometimes in the theatre, when the play is a familiar play of Shakespeare's, we may find ourselves no longer attentive, no longer listening. And then, perhaps, some line, or even some single phrase, will suddenly impress itself upon us, some line or phrase we had never noticed before. I recall a little speech of Desdemona's, a single line, in a performance of many years ago. It comes just after the dropping of the handkerchief when she and Othello are leaving the stage: 'I am very sorry that you are not well.' What struck me as I heard it then was the perfect simplicity of the words themselves, and equally the ease with which they were adjusted; the ease, that is, with which Shakespeare achieved a transition from one level of expression to another. The words were well spoken, too. 'Shakespeare', Sir John Gielgud remarked in an interview with the *Sunday Times* (1 October 1961), 'alternates stylized poetic imagery with natural intimate moments. The art of playing him lies in being exalted enough to deal with the poetry and relaxed enough to drop into the intimacy.'

There are times, however, when the transitions are abrupt, the contrasts in style strongly marked. Among scholars in the past these departures from the expected aroused suspicion and were often taken as evidence of multiple authorship. For Shakespeare, it was somehow assumed, must be all of a piece—and always at his best, or very nearly at his best. That there might be reasons of a compelling sort, dramatic reasons, for such shifts in style was too often ignored. Now a fairly general change in our approach to such passages has occurred in recent years. Things, meanings, in the suspect passages have been discovered which had gone unperceived before. A closer reading of Shakespeare's text has been characteristic of the best criticism of recent years. (I confess I once referred to Time in *The Winter's Tale* as a 'dull old dog': I wouldn't dare to, or want to, now.) One notes that in several cases of this sort a transition to the supernatural is involved, and this transition is marked by music ('still' or 'solemn' music); and the dramatist may well have counted heavily upon the effect of this music—an effect lost to us as mere readers of the play.

The vision in *Cymbeline,* a long masque-like scene in the last act, is perhaps the most controversial of these doubted passages. I would make one point in its favour, a point which, perhaps, has not been made before. This is the difference in our attitude toward the play's denouement when, in performance, the vision is included. The presence of the supernatural makes acceptable what otherwise we condemn for its excess of coincidence, the too perfect solving of difficulty—an art no longer concealing art. *Cymbeline* is the hardest of any of the mature plays of Shakespeare to produce today.

A good deal has been written on problems raised by the Player's speech in *Hamlet,* and a measure of agreement has perhaps been reached on some of these. The heightening and violence of the style, with its sprinkling of queer words like 'bisson' and 'mobled', are thrown into relief by the prose which surrounds and even interrupts the speech. And it is praised (by Hamlet) and criticized (by Polonius). The shift in style is deliberate, then. Here what we are to feel is art, the art of the theatre, as against what we accept as reality. It is only when the dramatic setting and context of the speech are forgotten that Hamlet is accused, as for instance Professor

22

Harbage accuses him in his *Shakespeare's Audience,* of blaming the democratic elements in the audience for not appreciating what is in fact 'an outrageous example of bombast'. Steevens in the eighteenth century went so far as to suggest—seriously, it may be—that Hamlet's praise is part of his assumption of madness. Is it any wonder if actors have now and again yielded to temptation and so spouted the speech as to make it truly ridiculous? Given, on the contrary, with sincerity and a measure of skill it is still capable of producing what I take to be the right effect. So delivered, I have even known the speech to be applauded.

A reader of these plays, if he is at all imaginative, hears words spoken as he reads, the words sounding from the page; and often the voices of speakers are distinguishable one from another. 'A living character', T. S. Eliot writes in his essay on Massinger (he is thinking of characters in plays), 'is not necessarily "true to life". It is a person whom we can see and hear . . . The dramatist need not understand people; but he must be exceptionally aware of them.' The reality of many of Shakespeare's characters is brought home to us through our sense of hearing them—is ultimately a matter of style. Othello is an example, or Iago, or Gloster in *King Lear*; or, in the first part of *King Henry IV* not to go farther, Falstaff and Hotspur and the Hostess, perhaps even Bardolph, each of whom has an individual way of saying things— and Falstaff's very repetitions are unlike those of Mrs. Quickly.

At this point you may begin to wonder how far such distinctions may not be merely impressionistic, since they are indemonstrable. But first, criticism in Shakespeare's time was often concerned with such relationships between meaning and manner, as they exist, for instance, outside drama, in Spenser's *Shepheardes Calender*. And also, in the case of at least one of the characters whom I named a moment

23

ago, Hotspur, his tricks of speech are brought out and commented upon, at several times, by his uncle, his wife and the Prince of Wales, his rival; the last named in a mocking imitation of what we have just seen (and *heard*) for ourselves.

To go a step farther, Lady Macbeth has sometimes been described as having no ambition for herself but only (as a dutiful wife) for her husband. 'Imaginary splendours', Hudson remarked, have no allurement for her. Against this, there is what she says herself at the end of her first scene— and the sound of the words almost as much as their meaning:

> But you shall put
> This night's great business into my despatch,
> Which shall to all our nights and days to come
> Give solely sovereign sway and masterdom.

Bernard Shaw in a letter to Mrs. Patrick Campbell about her interpretation of this part wrote: 'When you play Shakespear, don't worry about the character, but go for the music . . . If you get the music right, the whole thing will come right.' And Lady Macbeth (he went on) 'says things that will set people's imagination to work if she says them in the right way.'

Looking back now, the changes of style in Shakespeare's plays frequently served dramatic purposes, or were related to character, a personal idiom. And in considering Lady Macbeth, we found that style became a means of correction to possible misinterpretation.

Not, of course, that style alone is enough to solve the problems or simplify the complexities of Shakespeare's characters. As evidence it may be inconclusive. There is the Prince of Morocco, for instance. Usually the part is played very seriously indeed, and his manner of speech seems in keeping with this view: a high style, with something of the strangeness and romance which we associate with the later

Moor of Venice. But is what he says accordingly exempt from ridicule?

> Even for that I thank you.
> Therefore I pray you lead me to the caskets
> To try my fortune. By this scimitar,
> That slew the Sophy and a Persian prince
> That won three fields of Sultan Solyman,
> I would o'erstare the sternest eyes that look,
> Outbrave the heart most daring on the earth,
> Pluck the young sucking cubs from the she-bear,
> Yea, mock the lion when'a roars for prey,
> To win thee, lady.

'By this scimitar' . . . he draws it, doesn't he? even, perhaps, flourishes it? (It was an actor's doing that, some years ago, which set me wondering.) And there are two things more which weigh against the dignified and somewhat pitiful Moor: the parallelism with Aragon (in fairy stories there will be, say, two bad sisters and one good one, or as here two clearly unacceptable lovers and then Bassanio) and Portia's dry remark at the close of the scene, 'Let all of his complexion choose me so.'

In Shakespearian characterization there are no simple equations. A villainous person may be endowed with eloquence and speak arrestingly even when there is no one present to deceive. Take that evil pair Suffolk and Margaret in the second part of *King Henry VI*. They speak as Elizabethan lovers might long to speak, or Elizabethan lyrical poets when they would express passion in terms of beauty:

> A wilderness is populous enough,
> So Suffolk had thy heavenly company;
> For where thou art, there is the world itself
> With every several pleasure in the world;
> And where thou art not, desolation.

The Shakespearian commentator, Thomas Peregrine Courtenay, writing in 1840, decided, indeed, that 'the beauty' here was 'not sufficient to overcome the disgust excited by the guilt of the parties'. But then the Victorians knew as well when not to be moved as when not to be amused.

I can think of no clearer example of a scene in which style must be taken into account in its interpretation than the scene of the gardeners in *Richard II*. Certainly they are not kin to the gravediggers in *Hamlet,* nor can one think of them as employable by Justice Shallow in Gloucestershire. What they say may pass as humanly conceivable; their manner of saying it is at several removes from reality:

MAN: Why should we, in the compass of a pale
         Keep law and form and due proportion,
         Showing, as in a model, our firm estate.
         When our sea-walled garden, the whole land,
         Is full of weeds, her fairest flowers chok'd up,
         Her fruit trees all unprun'd, her hedges ruined,
         Her knots disordered, and her wholesome herbs
         Swarming with caterpillars?

GARDENER: Hold thy peace.
         He that hath suffer'd this disordered spring
         Hath now himself met with the fall of leaf.

It is all 'distanced', as we say nowadays; and deliberately, beyond doubt. Shakespeare was quite capable of giving their speech a rustic reality had he chosen to do so. The attempts of Miss Margaret Webster, in her two productions of *Richard II* in New York, to force these characters into our world—through realistic intonations and the like—led only to incongruity and a sense that the actors were playing against the lines.

Boors, bumpkins and ninnies are without poetry in Shakespeare. The presence of even a touch of lyricism should make us reconsider our view of some character who had seemed to be one of these. I would cite the four lovers in *A Midsummer Night's Dream*, Helena and Hermia, Demetrius and Lysander. They are merely young lovers at the beginning, delightful as such, and they have plenty of poetry. It is poetry, too, of exactly the same sort Shakespeare himself wrote in many of his early sonnets: those first exchanges of Hermia and Lysander, for instance, on the course of true love's never running smooth: 'So quick bright things come to confusion.' Far from being absurd in themselves they become figures of fun only by moonlight in that same wood where even the Queen of Fairies must condescend to be amusing as she fondles the long ears of her beloved, finding him as wise as he is beautiful. *A Midsummer Night's Dream* is a poet's play. It is only travestied when this is forgotten by directors and critics who are insensitive to poetic style.

My last example of the possible uses of style as evidence of the relations between manner and meaning is from a tragedy. I refer to what Goneril and Regan say about their father's attendant knights in *King Lear*: that they are a crew of dangerous ruffians, a desperate train. Sometimes in the study, and lately on the stage, their word, the word of these monstrous women, has been taken against the King's; and the inference has been drawn, accordingly, that Goneril and Regan really had a sort of case against their father, that they were abused. Against their assertions is, however, the strongest sort of dramatic evidence.

First, when we see the sisters together, at the end of the long first scene in the play, they make it perfectly clear that they are planning to join forces, to conspire together, against their father. The passage, standing where it does for our understanding of what is to come, is expository. Secondly, later, Goneril's directions to Oswald preceding her clash with Lear prepare us for the use she makes of the behaviour of the knights as a pretext, as something to use against him. Again, later still, Regan asks whether Edgar was not 'companion with the riotous knights' and is answered by Edmund that 'he was of that consort!' And Edgar, one knows, is most unlikely to have associated himself with such men as Goneril and Regan describe. (While Edmund's statement may be a fabrication, in itself it is likely enough.) And, as if to clinch the matter, there is the evidence of style. After Oswald's insolence to him, the King sends one of these debauched ruffians to call the steward back. And the Knight returns.

KNIGHT: He says, my lord, your daughter is not well.

LEAR: Why came not the slave back to me when I
call'd him?

KNIGHT: Sir, he answered me in the roundest manner,
he would not.

LEAR: He would not?

KNIGHT: My lord, I know not what the matter is; but to my judgment your Highness is not entertain'd with that ceremonious affection as you were wont. There's a great abatement of kindness appears as well in the general dependants as in the Duke himself also and your daughter.

LEAR: Ha! say'st thou so?

KNIGHT: I beseech you pardon me, my lord, if I be mistaken; for my duty cannot be silent when I think your Highness wrong'd.

His manner of speech is conclusive: that of a man such as Lear describes, a man 'of choice and rarest parts', and one well acquainted 'with all particulars of duty'.

In the past, as I said, the dramatic functions of style were obscured by a too exclusive approach to style as evidence of authorship. More recently the subject has been a little neglected in our concentration on recurring themes and images. Our ears, too, have become somewhat dulled, it may be, to the subtleties of spoken verse.

August 1966

WILL THEY RIDICULE OUR SHAKESPEARE?

Bamber Gascoigne

One of the easiest ways of starting a lecture is by explaining a strange title: and the easiest way to explain mine is to tell you how I arrived at it. I'm here as a newspaper critic, and so Peter Smith asked me to say something about Shakespeare from the point of view of a practising journalist. But the problems facing a theatre critic on a newspaper are either too general (you are all unpublished critics) or too particular (very few of you are worrying about deadlines or problems of space) to make a good basis for a lecture. So I decided it would be more interesting to look into one very special problem, an extremely important one for critics and indeed for any serious member of the audience—the problem of adapting Shakespeare's plays. Almost every new production alters at various points the standard interpretation—if such a thing can ever be said to exist—of the play being performed, and so most productions are already to a certain limited extent 'adaptations'. Even the way a producer chooses to cut a play may contribute to this element of adaptation. And, though this happens less frequently, we have all seen Shakespearian productions where lines have been altered and even added. Can we then, as critics and members of the audience, find any usable standards by which to approve or condemn these various levels of deviation from our received texts?

The academic critic takes almost for granted a standard which is extremely easy to apply—that any deviation from the original is undesirable. But few newspaper critics would wish to take quite such an inflexible position. Consider for a moment the difference between the two. The academic critic sits in his timeless book-lined study, carefully, properly and usefully guarding the sacred texts. When news arrives of each new rape of his ward we expect him sooner or later to sally forth under the banner of purity and to lay powerfully about him.

But the newspaper critic was in at the very scene of the rape—a far more unbalancing experience. He was sitting there when the travesty first saw the bright lights of night, and like most of the audience around him he may well have been enjoying the outrage enormously. Within a couple of days (or in the case of many critics on daily papers, within forty-five minutes), he has to form and express his opinion on whether this latest way of treating Shakespeare was admirable, tolerable or outrageous. And make no mistake! it is he, or—let me re-identify myself—we, who are the patsies of the future. It is we who are going to be seen as expressing and partly forming the typical reaction of our modern audience. It is we who are going to be exhumed and read out at seminars like this, to ripples of merriment, in fifty or a hundred years' time. So—have we any chance of avoiding this fate? Can we set up standards which will give us a longer and yet not inflexible perspective on the adaptations we see?

This has become particularly relevant in England recently because we had, two years ago, an extremely successful adaptation combining the three parts of *Henry VI* with *Richard III* to make a trilogy under the title *The Wars of the Roses*. It was done by the Royal Shakespeare Company at the other Stratford upon the other Avon, and it seemed to me and to many others a great improvement on the original three plays of *Henry VI*. But it did contain whole passages and even scenes—and far more of them than most of the audience realized—which had been added by the adapter, John Barton. We laugh now at the adapters of the past for their ludicrous additions to Master William Shakespeare. The disturbing question, then, is: will future ages find our adaptations as humourously typical of our age as we find, say, Nahum Tate's and Davenant's humourously typical of the late seventeenth century? In other words, Will They Ridicule Our Shakespeare?

To try and set up a comparative standard, let's look briefly at some late seventeenth- and eighteenth-century adaptations. The most famous of all is Nahum Tate's *King Lear,* but Professor Mack outlined this admirably in his opening lecture so there is no need for me to dwell on it. Instead it might be interesting to sketch in something of the worst that has befallen our Festival plays this year during three and a half centuries of existence.

Julius Caesar suffered its most severe mauling at the hands of John Sheffield, Duke of Buckingham, in the early years of the eighteenth century. Like other cultivated gentlemen of his time, Buckingham was obsessed with the Unities, and his method of fitting *Julius Caesar* into their arbitrary strait jacket was a simple one. He turned it into two plays, *The Tragedy of Julius Caesar* and *The Death of Brutus.* Naturally this made necessary the equivalent of five acts of completely new material, but I suspect that from His Grace's point of view this was part of the scheme's appeal.

The first play fitted quite unresistingly into the alloted ration of twenty-four hours and one location, since, up to the outbreak of chaos after Antony's funeral oration, Shakespeare's plot takes place entirely in Rome and in a very tight sequence of time. The second play was less easy. It had to contain the battle of Philippi, but the scenes leading up to it could hardly all happen on or near the battlefield.

Buckingham's solution was to set the first three acts in Athens and the last two in Philippi, but he acknowledged freely that such irregularity required an apology:

> Our scene is Athens;
> But here our author besides other faults
> Of ill expressions and of vulgar thoughts
> Commits one crime that needs an act of grace
> And breaks the law of unity of place.

The Duke goes on to point out in his own defence that the Unity of Time is properly preserved—the play begins the day before Philippi and ends with the battle. He doesn't add that it was physically impossible for the characters to march from Athens to Philippi in the available time. And given the context, the objection is a valid one. Literalness breeds literalness.

While acknowledging his own 'ill expressions and vulgar thoughts', Buckingham nevertheless does his best to polish up some of Shakespeare's. So, in the place of one familiar line, we get, 'Friends, countrymen and Romans, hear me gently,' and of course here Buckingham is absolutely right. This was the age of Reason. Reason is almost by definition literal. And, again, once the mind is set on a literal course, 'lend me your ears' is most emphatically a vile phrase and a concept which opens up vistas of Bosch-like horrors.

I want to follow a little further this idea of altering specific phrases and words in keeping with the tastes or limitations of one's own time, but before doing so let's have a brief look at the equivalent worst fate of our other Festival play this year, *Henry IV*. The executioner this time was Philips, also in the early eighteenth century. He undertook such extensive alterations that a blow-by-blow account would be pointless, but a passage of his preface gives an idea of just how far this 'adaptation' went. He adopts a humble tone, saying that he does not wish to be in debt to so great a poet without acknow-ledgement, and there goes on to square the account.

> I desire my Readers will place to his Account, One or Two Hints and one Intire line in the 24th page . . . Four lines in the 38th page . . . Three Parts in Four of the Description of the Duke's dead Body, in page 71: And about Seventeen lines in the last scene.

These are vast structural adaptations and they are, of course, the exception to the rule in the history of Shakespearian adaptation. Each play will have suffered only one or two such travesties in its time, but there has been another much more continuous process of adaptation—that of emending specific words or phrases. I can't resist quoting you first of all my own favourite, a very familiar one which many of you will know already. It is in Davenant's version of *Macbeth*, dating from the time of the Restoration, where the lines,

> The devil damn thee black, thou cream-faced loon,
> Where got'st thou that goose look?

become, 'Now friend, what means thy change of counten-ance?' That again, splendid though it is, is too extreme and exceptional for our purposes but the same adaptation can provide another much more ordinary and more relevant example. In Shakespeare, Lady Macbeth prays for night, that her 'keen knife see not the wound it makes'. In Davenant the alteration is very slight. She merely prays that her 'keen steel see not the wound it makes'.

This is particularly interesting because Garrick, nearly a hundred years later, made the same alteration of 'knife' to 'steel' in *Romeo and Juliet* (in the line, 'And with this knife I'll help it presently'), and Dr. Johnson at much the same time was busily defending this very change of Davenant's. Johnson said that the feeling of terror is weakened by the name of an instrument used by butchers and cooks in the meanest employments; we do not immediately conceive that any crime of importance is to be committed with a knife: or who does not at last, from the long habit of connecting a knife with sordid offices, feel aversion rather than terror?

What more sordid office, one might ask, than killing Duncan?—but Johnson is thinking of both words in a more specifically menial sense than we are apt to. And the point is, if this is so, if Johnson and his contemporaries really felt 'aversion rather than terror' at the mention of a knife (and Johnson certainly had a far stronger stomach than most of the cultivated men of his time), then surely the only solution *was* to change 'knife' to 'steel'. It makes a telling comment on eighteenth-century society, but if that society could only respond to Shakespeare given the change, what other solution was there?

So this leads one to the idea of a principle of necessity in adaptation. Something of the same can be seen in Nahum Tate's famous *King Lear*. Tate in his preface says of his happy ending: 'Otherwise I must have encumbered the stage with dead bodies, which conduct makes tragedies conclude with unseasonable jests.' Again, if so, if it was really the only way of avoiding unseasonable jests, had he an alternative? And in Garrick's *Romeo and Juliet* there is another interesting and significant change. He upped Juliet's age from fourteen to eighteen, and I think this seems entirely valid when one remembers that his audience was the generation which was bringing up its daughters to behave like the young ladies in Jane Austen. Certainly the idea of Shakespeare's Juliet set loose in Jane Austen gives pause for thought.

These examples are very remote from us and it requires a special act of imagination to understand and perhaps condone the need for the alteration, but I can give you one which will strike nearer home. It was suggested to me in Stratford this week by John Pettigrew, and it's a line of Scarus's in the last act of *Antony and Cleopatra* when he is wounded in the battle but wants to emphasize that he can soldier on and take more cuts and gashes before he gives up. His way of saying this is:

> I have yet
> Room for six scotches more.

I think we may agree that a modern producer might justifiably take some liberties with this remark.

But the question arises: if we are not going to condemn out of hand every alteration, how can we distinguish the outrageous from the tolerable? I suggest that one can usefully divide adaptations into three categories.

The first consists of those adaptations that are right for their own time. Nahum Tate's *King Lear* was one of these, and indeed it remained right for a great many years after its own time—roughly from 1670 to 1840, which means that it has had a longer continuous run on the English stage than Shakespeare's own version. Another long-runner in this category would be Colley Cibber's *Richard III*, some lines of which Olivier dropped neatly into the lap of the cinema audience, as when he leaned from his horse, wheeling away to the battle of Bosworth after his night of guilty dreams, 'Richard's himself again.'

The second category contains adaptations which are right both for their own time and for the material. This, needless to say, is a very exclusive category. None of the seventeenth- or eighteenth-century adaptations which we have been discussing falls within it, but it is reasonable to say that several of Shakespeare's own plays are in this category. Such tragedies as *Hamlet* and *King Lear* were themselves adaptations of earlier and cruder plays, but adaptations which all of us here would agree to have been right both for their own time and for the material, and therefore probably for all time.

The third and last category is the trash-can for the failures, the monstrosities, the warped and laughable botches which are wrong both for their own time and the material. Buckingham's *Julius Caesar* was one of these, a ponderous academic exercise, a nonsense wrought by irrelevant rules of art. In a lesser way, and in only part of the play, even Garrick landed himself in this category when he cut the gravediggers' scene and almost the whole of the fifth act of *Hamlet*. He too followed the sensibilities of the learned— the contemporary Shakespearian editor George Steevens greatly praised the emendation—and in doing so produced something which was not only wrong for the play but even for his own audience. The prompter (recorded in Tate Wilkinson's memoirs) said that the change was 'greatly disliked by the million', and went on to add that 'no doubt your country squires would be for horse-whipping the actor that had struck out that natural scene of the grave-diggers'. For once, you'll probably agree, the country squires were right.

In the rest of this lecture I'd like to try and see how far we can judge our own century's attitudes and adaptations, using the seventeenth- and eighteenth-century examples as yard-sticks. I have deliberately left out the nineteenth century. The reason is that their interest in spectacle and in archae-ological exactitude—all of which takes time—resulted rather in cutting Shakespeare than in adapting him. It is also, in general terms, true to say that the nineteenth-century theatre was very little interested in the literary aspect of Shakespeare's plays and was much more obsessed with the problems and possiblilties of stagecraft and of physical surprise and magic in the playhouse. At its worst this interest led to a series of ludicrous gimmicks. To give you one extreme but very successful example, two American sisters, Kate and Ellen Bateman, toured America playing Shakespeare in 1850. They were so successful that Barnum brought them to London in 1851 where again they scored a tremendous hit. Their most popular successes were *Richard III*, in which Ellen played Richard and Kate, Richmond; and *The Merchant of Venice* in which they were Shylock and Portia. At the height of their fame Kate's age was eight, Ellen's six.

So the nineteenth century, whether at its most serious or its most ridiculous, is in a very real sense separate from the centuries before and after it. Both the eighteenth and twentieth centuries have had a serious interest in Shakespeare's plays. Their reasons for adapting him have been similar in kind, though very different in detail. Roughly it would be true to say that the eighteenth century adapted Shakespeare to appease such household gods as the Unities (Buckingham's *Julius Caesar*), Decorum (no cream-faced loons), Poetic Justice (Cordelia has to live) and Balance (Nahum Tate provided a lover for Cordelia; Davenant counter-poised Miranda with a man who had never seen a woman, and even provided a ghost for Lady Macbeth—'equal apparitions for women', as Robertson Davies commented rather aptly at these seminars three years ago). One could list several more such 'principles', but these have emerged from the examples we have discussed.

Our reasons are vastly different and in a few moments I want to look into them in as much detail as we have time for. The interesting question is whether they are any better. Put in most general terms the difference is between adapting for aesthetic reasons (the eighteenth century) and for considerations of meaning (ourselves). In other words where they were aiming for Balance, we tend to alter for the sake of Clarity. Where they were on the trail of Beauty, we are addicts of Significance.

I would like to look at this in two modern adaptations, one of them the worst and one the best that I have ever come across. I'll begin with the worst because I want to spend less time on it (critics actually prefer dwelling on what is good, though the public will never believe this). I also want to get it over with because it's most alarming to have to say in this building—I'm not even sure that the walls will stand passively while I do so—that this worst adaptation in my own theatre-going experience was Sir Tyrone Guthrie's of *The Alchemist* at the Old Vic three or four years ago. *The Alchemist* of of course is not Shakespeare, but Ben Jonson was an exact contemporary and in any case these elusive principles that we are seeking would have to apply equally well to classics of any period.

Guthrie's intention in adapting the text of *The Alchemist* was to point up its relevance to modern life and so prevent the audience from seeing the play's parable as a quaint charade from another time with no reference to themselves. Most of you will remember the plot, but to outline it very briefly: it concerns three con men who claim to be on the verge of discovering the philosopher's stone, which by alchemy can turn any material into gold and in this case is supposed to be able to effect almost any other piece of magic that may be desired. They're visited by a flock of greedy fools who are duly fleeced, and the great merit of the situation for Jonson is that it enables him to present a splendid procession of satirized characters in the grips of every type of fashionable gullibility.

The fallacy of Guthrie's attitude, which in this century has been an extremely prevalent one, lies in thinking that the real relevance of any fable resides in its trappings, and that it can therefore be brought up to date by altering such surface matters as clothes, props, place names or quirks of contemporary jargon. Guthrie himself expressed half the real truth in a programme note to this production, where he

38

explained his reasons for all the inserted gobbets of modernity but at the same time pointed out that he hadn't needed to alter the central detail of the philosopher's stone because any fool should be able to think of equivalents in the modern world. He gave an example of some relations of his who handed over all their money to a trickster to invest in a gold mine of fabulous prospects; they heard no more of him or it. In this Guthrie is entirely right, and for a modern Ben Jonson, writing an entirely new *Alchemist,* a sharp stock-broker might well be a strong candidate for the central role. (Actually modern life outdid Jonson in his own field this summer in New York, where the police reports included a story of some con men who had deprived two Dixieland farmers of 25,000 dollars by borrowing the money to feed into a magic black box which produced two ten-dollar bills for every one that was put in.)

Yet Guthrie, having seen this essential point about the audience's ability to identify the philosopher's stone, then solemnly sets about turning 'coach-and-six' into 'limousine'. Can he seriously believe that anyone who could see a stockbroker in an alchemist might fail to see a limousine in a coach-and-six? What is genuinely hard to imagine is somebody visiting an alchemist in a limousine, which is precisely what Guthrie ended up with.

The two foremost sufferers at Guthrie's hands were Kastril and his sister Dame Pliant. In Jonson, Kastril is a young *nouveau riche* from the provinces with 3,000 pounds a year who wants to be taught the etiquette of quarrelling so that he can become on of the 'angry boys'. He also wants to marry his sister to a peer. Guthrie seems to have made some sort of very superficial connection between 'angry boys' and modern teenage gangs, with the result that in his version Kastril rides a motorbike and wears, like his sister behind him on the pillion, a crash helmet and a suit of hideous black leather. As for quarrelling in the approved fashion (a very important matter which Touchstone in *As You Like It* is also obsessed with), all that Kastril now wants from the alchemists is to be provided with a flick-knife. However, he still wants his sister to marry a peer, and his income—in keeping with modern inflation—has been raised to 20,000 pounds per annum.

The result of all this is the complete absence of any sort of sociological relevance, whether past or present. Jonson's play, if allowed to be consistent to itself, has an unmistakable and timeless relevance for us all. Guthrie, in trying to improve on this, only succeeded in eradicating it. Buckingham with his eye on the rules of art failed to catch any sort of eighteenth-century reality. Guthrie, focusing in a similar way on Significance, misses the twentieth-century mark and lands himself firmly in our third category, with an adaptation that is wrong both for its material and for its own time. Believe it or not, people determined to marry a peer are now almost as rare in England as those with 60,000 dollars a year on motorbikes.

I should add here that one or two of Guthrie's minor verbal alterations were far more defensible, rather in the same way as the changes from 'knife' to 'steel' in the eighteenth century. For example, he altered the word 'loadstone' to 'magnet' in a line which would have been incomprehensible to anyone not knowing what a loadstone was. Purists will point out that the texture of the verse is affected by such a change, but I think that this can often be a price worth paying for comprehension. I say 'can often', sounding perhaps unduly cautious, because I believe we tend to set too high a premium on the understanding of every single word in a theatrical performance; and in doing so we misunderstand what happens in the mind of an audience when it watches a play.

There was a very relevant example of this recently in England, when the National Theatre did a production of *Much Ado About Nothing* and employed Robert Graves to alter some three hundred phrases which were considered obscure. This inevitably caused quite an outcry, but the proper objection to the alterations seemed to me that they were unnecessary rather than that they must automatically be wrong. It happened that Robert Graves's version at times almost added to any existing obscurity, but my point is that some obscurity in the original text is totally unimportant. In the vast variety of feelings, images and ideas which pass through the mind of a spectator watching a play, many phrases will not be fully or properly understood; and at the same time—the other side of the coin—many implications which are not there will strike him with force and often with pleasure.

I remember—again to use one of our Festival plays—that I as a boy enjoyed a splendid misunderstanding of this sort about *Julius Caesar* which, as no doubt for many of you here, was one of the first Shakespeare plays I read. For many years I went about with the happy conviction that Caesar, for his dying words, burst into French—'Et tu, Brute?' The odd thing was I was not at all disturbed at the idea of his speaking French, but was rather distressed that he should have got his grammar so lamentably wrong. I knew that 'toi aussi' would have been ideal, but after all even 'et toi' would have done and would not have disturbed the scansion. However, I did appreciate that this for Caesar was a moment of great stress, etc., etc. But the interesting thing is that the budding critic in me was enormously impressed at the way in which Shakespeare, by using French at this point, had been able to bring in an extremely powerful and relevant pun—with Caesar validly calling his treacherous friend 'brute'. So you see something of the value of creative misunderstandings. Long live the minor obscurities!

But to come to my second example—the best modern adaptation of an Elizabethan play that I have seen. It was the recent adaptation that I mentioned earlier of all three parts of *Henry VI* combined with *Richard III* into a trilogy, *The Wars of the Roses,* which was first presented at Stratford-upon-Avon in 1963. The adapter, John Barton, made a great number of alterations, excisions and, most important and interesting, additions. But I think the simplest way of analysing what he was trying to do, and how far he was justified, is by looking at the single most drastic and most effective new element in his adaptation.

This was the addition of two non-Shakespearian details in the council scenes. In Shakespeare these council scenes, throughout the three parts of *Henry VI*, form a rather muddled series of meetings between the various noblemen jockeying for power. The young king's regent, the Duke of Gloucester, is at the start indisputably the most powerful among them all. Early on in Shakespeare he is accused of usurping too much power for himself. He denies the charge, and at this point Barton makes his first crucial addition. His Gloucester, as a token of his own lack of personal ambition, suggests that in future the council should conduct its business by a show of hands with the decision going to the majority, with the king of course having a power of absolute veto or control if he wishes to exercise it. One result of this addition is that the shifting patterns of power are made much clearer in each of the council scenes by the visible show of hands, but an even more dramatic result is achieved in the scene of Gloucester's impeachment.

In Shakespeare, Gloucester is impeached with scanty arguments, is arrested and is hurried away. The king makes one brief speech of a non-intervention. He is clearly failing his deputy, but in theatrical terms he does so almost as if from the side lines, through silence. Barton reserves for this scene various accusations against Gloucester from earlier parts of Shakespeare's play, thus making the case against Gloucester much clearer, and at the same time his innovations in council procedure result in a far more pointed crisis than Shakespeare provides. First the vote has to go against Gloucester—a series of mailed fists lowered to the table—but even then Gloucester is able to turn to his king and remind him of his power of veto. Within this framework the king's failure to save him becomes far stronger, and of course requires a more substantial speech which Barton, like Buckingham before him, is happy to provide. However, unlike Buckingham, he admires the basic nature of Elizabethan blank verse and in the middle of the rather journeyman poetry of these plays he is able to insert his own lines without anyone but a serious student of the text being likely to recognize which is which.

So what Barton has done is to take a series of elements and themes which are undoubtedly present in a somewhat jumbled and repetitive form in Shakespeare's trilogy, and to present them with a refined clarity and sharpness. I personally found the result enormously successful and so, it seemed, did most members of the audience. There were of course objections from those who feel that any alteration of Shakespeare is wrong and that we should by now have learned our lesson from the past; but I hope I have suggested that this may be too rigid a position.

There were also objections about Barton's lack of historical accuracy. One of the first critics to speak against the trilogy was Kenneth Muir who complained in the *Guardian* about the unhistorical intrusion of a majority vote in the king's council. But how much does this matter? And how historical is Shakespeare himself? Hector in *Troilus and Cressida*, name-dropping to his brothers, can clamly invoke the name of Aristotle. In *Henry VI*, Part 3, the Duke of Gloucester, the future Richard III, proudly boasts that he can 'set the murderous Machiavel to school' in a year when Machiavelli was aged precisely two. I firmly believe that when we are watching a play the theatre's own built-in laws transcend the precise demands of history.

When I told him that I was going to give this lecture and thought of discussing *The Wars of the Roses,* John Barton very kindly lent me his notes for the adaptation, many of which were in the form of letters to the director, Peter Hall, during the planning stage. They reveal many interesting points about the specifically modern attitudes behind the adaptation, and I think it's well worth quoting from a few of them. In one of his letters Barton wrote:

> I don't think we can make a good play out of a bad one, but we can at least inform a pedestrian narrative plot with some complexity of human relationship. I think we can also cut down the personal brawling a good deal further. In its place I think we should get much more political content. The lords should not thrash about in vacuo but in a concrete political, economic and military crisis.

Not 'in vacuo but in a concrete political, economic and military crisis'. This particular desire is a very familiar one in modern theatre, largely owing to the powerful influence of Brecht—in my opinion a good influence, but one very particularly of our time. Or again:

> In further revising the text I should like to establish a parallel with the curse on the House of Atreus, which would help enormously to raise Margaret's railings in Part C [i.e., *Richard III*] from the petty to the cosmic.

Another very familiar twentieth-century attitude, a little earlier than the Brechtian—the conviction that we can somehow take on something of the cosmic grandeur of

44

Greek drama by rubbing shoulders with its themes, a conviction that ruined most of the middle years of work of a dramatist as powerful as Eugene O'Neill and that led T. S. Eliot to hope that he could perhaps combine significance and box-office appeal by smuggling the Furies into the drawing-room. A third extract provides a less specifically Grecian version of the same general attitude: 'The lawyer maintains the dynasty theme, the lieutenant the Tower theme, Margaret the curse theme.' This is the approach of many a modern playwright—to think, even before beginning to write, in terms of themes, both for the sake of clarity and for the supposed weight which such an approach is expected to bring.

These quotations reveal only a mental attitude, dug out a little unfairly from notes, and it is to the enormous credit of the Barton adaptation that such conscious modern attitudes were so successfully buried and hidden in the final version. Part of the success of the whole production may well be that such fashionable themes were present without seeming in any way superimposed. They appeared an entirely integral part of the material.

The Wars of the Roses is not yet published. When it is available, I suspect that it may spread far as the standard way of doing the three parts of *Henry VI,* and so become something of a Nahum Tate *King Lear* or Colley Cibber *Richard III* in terms of holding the stage. I am even tempted to think that it may qualify for my select second category, an adaptation which is right both for its own time and for the material. Or will later ages perhaps find the twentieth-century attitudes which it undoubtedly contains more blatant and more extraneous than we do, and so come to regard it as a Nahum Tate *King Lear* in the other sense? Here is perhaps the best possible context for my original question—will they ridicule our Shakespeare? Time alone will tell.

45

One thing, though, I hope that I have convinced you of—
that adaptations must be judged individually on their own
merits. There can be no law about what may or may not be
adapted or how far one can go. The only possible yardstick
is what Shakespeare himself meant or may have meant, and
fortunately there is no one answer to this and never can be.
Any interpretation of this sort must always in the end be
subjective. There's a good example of this in a passage by
Robert Speaight in his *William Poel and the Elizabethan
Revival* which demonstrates well how dangerous it is to
insist on an absolute interpretation of any play. Speaight is
ridiculing the idea that a Shakespeare play can hold a special
meaning for each new age and says, among other examples,
that such absurd notions

> have led in New York to a modern dress *Julius Caesar*
> [he is referring to Orson Welles's of 1937] where a play
> designed to show the havoc wrought by high-minded
> liberals, caught in the toils of their own demagogy, is
> treated as anti-Fascist propaganda.

Not only is his dogmatic account of Shakespeare's intention
open to very serious dispute, but interestingly enough his
very choice of phrases—'high-minded liberals' and so on—
reveals a purely twentieth-century cast of thought. I repeat—
fortunate as it is for those of us who work as critics, we can
never come up with any final version of what Shakespeare
meant.

Of course—to offer you a slight diversion—we can always
go for the answer to the two books that Shakespeare wrote
after he had finished his life's work, books in which he set
down exactly what he did mean. I see some of you sitting
up in mild surprise—understandably, since these are certainly
not among his better known writings. In fact neither was
published until this century and both were dictated through
mediums; and certainly both books are very charming, even

46

if academically a little unreliable. One of them, published in 1919 (*Shakespeare's Revelations by Shakespeare's Spirit* through medium of S. T. Shatford) has this splendid affidavit on the title page:

> Dictated exactly as found herein. No illiteracies, no obliterations, chargeable to the Medium. My hand and seal hereon. W. S. in Spirit.

The other, published in the 1940s (*Elizabethan Episode* by Daisy O. Roberts), will be particularly useful to members of this seminar who have spent a lot of time this week in discussing the ambiguities of *Julius Caesar*. Shakespeare dictated several passages on *Caesar,* with such revealing comments as:

> I loved Brutus and tried to make him good all the time. Perhaps I overdid my whitewashing for he seems now, I see, to be rather more despicable than Cassius.

This second book is full of reincarnation. Shakespeare was, it turns out, Ovid, but was not Homer. And some of the familiar but more homely problems are happily cleared up:

> My second best bed? That's all right: it was as good only small. She would have everything else she wanted.

But to return from the free-wheeling realms of spiritualism, can we come up with any sort of verdict as between the eighteenth century and ourselves in terms of our attitude to Shakespeare and to adapting him? In the eighteenth century's favour it is worth emphasizing, since a great many witty words in books, articles and lectures have been devoted to ridicule of their adaptation, that though most of their texts were 'bad' to some extent, nevertheless the bulk of almost all of them was still Shakespeare. So they saw, in a sense, considerably more Shakespeare than we do. The number of actual Shakespeare productions available to the tiny playgoing

47

audience of eighteenth-century London was, by our modern standards, very large indeed. David Nichol Smith has pointed out in *Shakespeare in the Eighteenth Century* that in the year of *The Beggar's Opera* (1728) the London playgoer could see *Hamlet, Othello, King Lear, Macbeth,* both parts of *Henry IV, The Merry Wives of Windsor, Richard III, Henry VIII* and *Julius Caesar*; and in the year of *She Stoops to Conquer* (1773) the choice was even greater: *Hamlet, Othello, King Lear, Macbeth, Romeo and Juliet, Richard III, Henry VIII, Julius Caesar, The Merchant of Venice, As You Like It, Much Ado About Nothing, Twelfth Night, Cymbeline* and *The Tempest.*

In our favour it is true to say that where the eighteenth century knew it was better than Shakespeare, we only think we are like him. And to a limited extent we are right in thinking so. Between his age and ours there has been not other period of such rapid social change or of such violence, and the feeling of identity is clearly reflected in such things as the English title of the recent very widely read book by the Polish professor, Jan Kott: *Shakespeare, Our Contemporary.*

But even if we have some cause for this feeling, it may well be an area in which the future will find our claims both presumptuous and somewhat hilarious. For example, it is likely to seem a little topsy-turvy that Professor Kott should energetically analyse *Lear* in terms of Samuel Beckett's *Endgame,* even though this very analysis had the excellent practical result of inspiring Peter Brook's production of *Lear* with Paul Scofield a couple of years ago. Or again, essay headings like Raymond Southall's 'Troilus and Cressida and the Spirit of Capitalism' may seem strange. In each case there is validity in the comparison, but the approach may soon appear unduly warped—too much remaking the master in our own image. Or how about all those producers of *Hamlet* who are so visibly grateful that a man as busy as Shakespeare should have devoted so much time to reading

Freud? All these may be possible grounds for future merriment.

But even so I think that we are likely to be slightly less ridiculed, with the emphasis perhaps on 'slightly', than the eighteenth century has been. We have, to protect us, two safeguards, the second rather more admirable than the first. The first is the modern cult of originality, whereby we are all perpetually crying out to be amazed with something new. This leads to a great deal of rubbish, but does mean that should any ludicrous version of a Shakespeare play become the present-day norm it will only be a very short time before the wheel has turned full circle and it is again new and exciting to do the play as Shakespeare wrote it. The second safeguard is that since the turn of the last century we profess to have, and in most cases do have, a genuine concern with the text. John Barton swears that he would not meddle with the mature plays (though I am not sure that Tyrone Guthrie would swear the same), and undoubtedly Barton's treatment of the three parts of *Henry VI* is made much more widely acceptable by the fact that they are such early plays and are in general so little admired for themselves.

The problem of where the major plays can be said to begin is large enough for another whole lecture, but so as not to be accused of shirking it entirely I would repeat that I don't believe any one hard and fast line can be drawn in these matters. I myself would look with very kindly eyes on anyone who had the outrageous temerity to meddle with the last scenes of *Romeo and Juliet*. In fact I believe that if Shakespeare had written the ending of *West Side Story,* in which Romeo is killed by a relative of Juliet's and the girl's grief over his corpse suddenly brings the warring factions to their senses, and if some later hack, obsessed with gothic horrors and nonsensical coincidence, had tacked on Shakespeare's ending of intercepted messages, magic potions and moonlit tombs, then we should all, and rightly, rise in furious protest at such a travesty of our great Himself.

This is of course to provoke you, but I also mean it; and it is worth pointing out at the end of the lecture that it is the very adaptability of Shakespeare that has been one of the basic causes of his continued success. Amazing though it sounds to state it in such terms, he has been England's most popular playwright at every moment since six or seven years after his first play appeared, and has also been the world's most popular playwright for much of that time; and part of the reason is that everyone has always been able to find his own in Shakespeare. The plays in each context have seemed so nearly what was wanted that it was worth bridging the gap and adapting them. To see what I mean you only have to compare a dramatist like Racine—superb but within such precise limits that you either have to accept him on his own terms or not at all. Adaptation is unthinkable. His drama is essentially a delicate wine which will not travel, whereas Shakespeare has travelled not only through all periods since his own but also throughout the entire world. Miss Bradbrook tells me that when she went on a tour of the Far East in the centenary year she found an interest in Shakespeare even in remote Indonesian villages where nothing else at all was known about English or European literature.

Just to leave you with one nice, frivolous and really way-out example of Shakespearian adaptation—how pleasant to find *The Merchant of Venice* popping up in Japan, in 1877, under the splendid and alluring title: *The Strange Affair of the Flesh of the Bosom.*

August 1965

SHAKESPEARE STUDY TODAY

John Russell Brown

The pace of scholarship is snail-like, and criticism is usually concerned with minor adjustments of opinion, not with turning upside down. In both, new detail, new terminology, new shadings or extensions to a generally accepted picture, are eagerly sought for and patiently substantiated. All this is proper for pursuits in which judgement and responsibility are inevitably required.

But today in Shakespeare studies there is, I think, a dramatic situation: significant changes are discernible, new attitudes, new subjects for study; and a new admission of ignorance.

At any time in the last two decades, it would have been fairly comprehensive to say that there were two main lines of study. The earlier attention to character and consideration of Shakespeare's development as a man and artist—the poet providing a pattern for sensitive men in a hero-dominated world—had given way to more painstaking studies: I shall call them 'deductive analysis' and 'historical reconstruction'.

The analysers took their cue from critics of short poems and a new interest in linguistic ambiguity. They examined small, usually verbal elements from a play in order to discover their constitution, and then used their findings as indications of the constitution of the whole. There was, for example, a whole series of books that discussed something called 'Shakespeare's imagery'. The first major contribution in this line was Caroline Spurgeon's *Shakespeare's Imagery and What It Tells Us* (1935). Miss Spurgeon took each play in turn and made lists of the metaphors and similes used in them; and she found that each play had its own set of dominant images. She was most concerned to use this analysis to reconstruct the 'mind' of Shakespeare, what people, ideas and things he responded to at different stages of his career. So she reported that he disliked dogs, but loved outdoor sports; that he was short of cash in the middle of his life, and so forth. But her description of dominant images in individual works had the greatest influence: the prevalence of beast images in many social plays, cosmic, global, mythic ones in *Antony and Cleopatra,* images of corruption in *Hamlet,* and so forth.

Professor Clemen of Munich followed with his *Development of Shakespeare's Imagery* in 1936, and now the study of imagery could go hand-in-hand with the verbal acuity of two Cambridge critics, W. W. Empson and I. A. Richards—the last chiefly known for his *Practical Criticism,* or his *Principles of Literary Criticism,* in which by far the longest chapter is called 'The Analysis of a Poem'. Empson's *Seven Types of Ambiguity* (1930) had discussed Shakespeare as a poet, alongside untheatrical writers like Donne, Herbert, Marvell, Keats, early T. S. Eliot and others, but *The Structure of Complex Words* of 1951 analyses the use of significant words in single plays, as the imagists had discussed their dominant images: here are essays on 'fool' in *Lear,* 'honest' in *Othello,* 'sense' in *Measure for Measure.* In the same tradition is M. M. Mahood's *Shakespeare's Word-Play* (1957) which has chapters on individual plays approached through detailed study of their puns.

Less rigorous in procedure, but also interested in recurrent imagery and words, was G. Wilson Knight. *The Wheel of Fire: Essays in Interpretation of Shakespeare's Sombre Tragedies*

(1930) and *The Shakespearean Tempest* (1932) were the first of a series of books, not yet completed, which analyse the 'poetry' to discover the 'shaping ideas' behind the writing of the plays. In an introduction to his second book, Wilson Knight explained that he thought his approach reached the 'heart' of the plays:

> While we view the plays primarily as studies in character, abstracting the literary person from the close mesh of that poetic fabric into which he is woven, we shall . . . end by creating a chaos of the whole. If, however, we give attention always to poetic colour and suggestion first, thinking primarily in terms of symbolism, not 'characters', we shall find each play in turn appear more and more amazing in the delicacy of its texture, and then, and not till then, will the whole of Shakespeare's work begin to reveal its rich significance, its harmony, its unity.

He drew up a chart showing the 'real lines of force in Shakespeare', how the 'basic symbols of tempest and music in vital opposition unify Shakespeare's world.' So key words, taken out of poetic and dramatic context, are arranged on a page, 'Bright' at the top and 'Dark' at the foot; in between these are music, tempests, battles, cannon, drums, silence. Across the page, run 'royalty' and 'love', 'warrior honour' and 'religious grace', or 'weird women', 'ghosts' and 'madness'.

In all these books a study of words and imagery has led to a study of 'themes', the conceptions (or 'meanings', or 'structure' of thought) that link the various elements together. Two highly sensitive contributions in this kind, whose titles speak for their contents directly, are R. B. Heilman's *This Great Stage: Image and Structure in 'King Lear'* (1948) and L. C. Knights's *Some Shakespearean Themes* (1959), the latter considering themes such as 'Time', 'Nature' and 'appearance

53

and reality' through a number of plays. In his first chapter, Knights echoed both Wilson Knight and Empson:

> The verse has moved well into the centre of the picture. . . . Meanings from below the level of 'plot' and 'character' take form as a living structure . . . closely connected with recurring and inter-related imagery.

He summed up on *King Lear* like this:

> Our seeing has been directed towards . . . nothing less than *what man is*. The imaginative discovery that is the play's essence has thus involved the sharpest possible juxtaposition of rival conceptions of 'Nature'.

Instead of trying to describe what happens in a play in terms of character and plot—an activity which is bound to be impressionistic and apt to yield only a paraphrase of Shakespeare's text—Knights analysed recurrent words to expose their connections and inter-relations; his Shakespeare is conceptual, sharp, highly organized.

Deductive analysis of this kind varies from brilliant raids upon the verbal texture of a play to elaborate and slow-footed commentary. Derek Traversi's later books, such as *Shakespeare: The Last Phase* (1954) or *Shakespeare from 'Richard II' to 'Henry V'* (1958), are so close-packed, so concerned to dissect multiple meanings within individual words and to note recurrences and relationships, that they do not so much interpret the plays as immerse the readers in endlessly minute sifting of words and images. One of the difficulties about deductive analysis is its great wealth of material—after the critic has lost faith in his discovery of *the* important or comprehensive elements for dissection. While discussing clear-cut themes in a comparatively small number of plays, L. C. Knights protected himself from this danger by claiming that he studied only '*some*' of the Shakespearian themes.

54

The other school, dominant for at least twenty years, was that of historical reconstruction. The object here was to read the plays from an Elizabethan point of view, to study the prejudices, attitudes and ideology of Shakespeare's contemporaries and so recover references and statements in the plays that had been obscured by time. Perhaps the most influential book in this line of study was E. M. W. Tillyard's *Shakespeare's History Plays* (1944). The idea came to the critic during the Second World War, when nationalistic sentiments had current force; but before he was able to write his book, Tillyard found it necessary to write another: *The Elizabethan World Picture,* published a year earlier. Here the Tudor historians and homiletic propagandists speak for themselves and present an 'Elizabethan' view of politics and society, and only when this task was done did Tillyard proceed to show the reflection of these ideas in Shakespeare's history plays. Instead of being rather awkward and inconvenient backgrounds for a number of brilliant portraits—Falstaff, Richard II, the Bastard, etc.—the histories became meaningful in plan and detail as well; they had 'Elizabethan' meaning. Shakespeare was like a homilist:

> In the total sequence of his plays dealing with the subject matter of Hall [the Chronicler], he expressed successfully a universally held and still comprehensible scheme of history; a scheme fundamentally religious, by which events evolve under a law of justice and under the ruling of God's Providence, and of which Elizabeth's England was the acknowledged outcome.

Many other scholars were turning into critics with similar effect. In the United States, Lily B. Campbell had published, as early as 1930, her *Shakespeare's Tragic Heroes: Slaves of Passion,* in which a reading of Renaissance books about the nature of man—a creature ruled by reason or by passion—enabled her to see Shakespeare's characters as examples of the ill-effects of immorality. Professor Campbell's later study, *Shakespeare's 'Histories': Mirrors of Elizabethan Policy* (1947), argued that these plays reflected not merely the current political theories but also actual events from Elizabeth's England: their historical names often disguised representations of Mary Queen of Scots, Leicester, Essex, or the Queen herself.

The sensibility of less sophisticated Elizabethans has also been studied by the Shakespearian critics. So the 'folk' element in the plays has recently been stressed. The most ambitious book of this sort, and one of the earliest, is Colin Still's *Shakespeare's Mystery Play* or *The Timeless Theme* (1936): for this Frazer's *Golden Bough* has been put to service and *The Tempest* read in great detail in a search for echoes of fertility, initiation and other popular rites; the whole play becomes a re-enactment or celebration. Twenty years later, C. L. Barber used a more restrictedly Elizabethan study to see the earlier comedies in the same way. His *Shakespeare's Festival Comedy* (1959) argues that

> Shakespeare's fundamental method [in writing romantic comedies from Italianate sources] was to shape the loose narrative so that events put its persons in the position of festive celebrants.

Twelfth-night revelry, midsummer madness, and the rites of May, Robin Hood and the golden age, masked dances, killing the deer, and so forth, were here recognized main structural members rather than incidental decorations. So, Professor Barber argued, Elizabethans would have received them.

Recently John Holloway, in *The Story of the Night* (1961), has effected the same sort of restoration process on the tragedies; he presented the hero, not as a flawed master-man nor as a slave of passion, but as a scapegoat ceremoniously isolated from society and by his death sustaining society.

Many writers have recovered a specifically 'Christian' Shakespeare speaking within the religious tradition of his age. S. L. Parker, Robert Speaight, P. N. Seigel, Roland Mushat Frye are among this band. Irving Ribner on *King Lear* in his *Patterns in Shakespearian Tragedy* (1960) can exemplify: for him characters become 'figures':

> Edgar becomes a symbol of divine justice triumphing over evil to reassert the harmony of God's natural order. The blast of his trumpet as he goes into combat is a symbolic echo of the last judgement. . . . Cordelia cannot be judged by any standard of psychological verisimilitude. . . . She is not a real person. . . . She serves like the earlier Desdemona, as a symbol of love and self sacrifice, a reflection of the love of God.

The two schools of criticism have one attitude in common: both look for a 'meaning'. Whether he works by examining small, verbal elements or by searching for indications of Elizabethan attitudes, the critic tries to 'interpret' or 're-interpret'. Some write about a previously concealed 'structure' or 'pattern of thought': L. C. Knights has appropriated Henry James's metaphor of the 'pattern in the carpet'; and 'character' and 'development' have been taken as part of the surface of things, behind which there is 'meaning'.

The titles of critical studies of Shakespeare published within the last twenty or twenty-five years demonstrate this common concern: *An Interpretation of Shakespeare*; *Shakespeare's Doctrine of Nature*; *The Meaning of Shakespeare*—(notice '*The* Meaning'); *As They Liked It*—(that sounds less rigorous, but a subtitle follows)—*an Essay on Shakespeare and Morality*; *The Sense of Shakespeare's Sonnets*; *Shakespeare and the Nature of Man*; *Shakespeare's World of Images*—(again a wider aim; but again there is a subtitle)—*the Development of his Moral Ideas*; *Shakespeare and the Natural Condition*; *Justice and Mercy in Shakespeare*; *Shakespearian Tragedy and the Elizabethan Compromise*; *Shakespeare's Tragic Justice*; *The Philosophy of Shakespeare*; *Shakespeare and Christian Doctrine*; *The Problem Plays of Shakespeare*; *Shakespeare and the Allegory of Evil*. It is this basic interest that is being questioned now. There is, I think, a growing realization that a man is not only what he thinks he believes, but also what he does; he is not only what he thinks in common with others of his generation, not only what words he uses, but also *how* he lives. And with these attitudes to ourselves, there are new attitudes to art: a work of art is not only what it ostensibly says it means, nor what we may deduce that its author meant; we must try to consider what a poem, a painting or a play does—not give our primary attention to what it says.

Uneasiness with the pursuit of Shakespeare's 'meaning' has been expressed on several sides. Robert Ornstein's *The Moral Vision of Jacobean Tragedy* (1960) is in title and organization within the 'meaning-seeking' tradition, but during the course of the book and especially in a brilliantly self-critical opening chapter, there are warnings against its own method. First Professor Ornstein explains that we cannot 'know' the cultural background of the plays: an 'intellectual montage' of ideas that is 'perfectly accurate in every detail' would be perfectly misleading in its impression of static homogeneity'; it is one thing to know what was in the books that dramatists and their audiences read, and quite another to know what they were able and willing to read in them. He refuses to mark the boundaries or landmarks of an imaginary and theatrical world with the measures of an intellectual one: 'Within the drama', he writes, 'there is no pattern of intellectual resolution, nor a continuing interest in specific ethical questions.' He looks for a 'positive note', but sometimes says he cannot find one. He begins to consider what a play does:

And, in fact, to attempt to define Hamlet's character by weighing his motives and actions against any system of Renaissance thought is to stage *Hamlet* morally without the Prince of Denmark, i.e., without the *felt impression* of Hamlet's moral nature. . . .

Only if we surrender ourselves to the *moods* of the individual plays . . . can we 'know' the ethics of the tragedies.

In speaking of a 'felt impression' or 'mood', Professor Ornstein acknowledges that 'interpretation' must wait upon the hitherto unfashionable 'appreciation'.

In a provoking and considered article in *Shakespeare Quarterly* (1960), Clifford Leech has written of 'The "Capability" of Shakespeare' and so summoned Keats for comparison. He refers, of course, to Keats's notion of a poet's 'negative capability':

that is when a man is capable of being in uncertainties, mysteries, doubts, without any irritable reaching after fact and reason.

If Keats is right in supposing that a great poet lives by sensations rather than thought and is therefore able to live in uncertainties, are we not foolish to look for a 'meaning' in Shakespeare, especially 'the' meaning of Shakespeare?

We cannot legitimately regard the plays as we regard non-dramatic writings. We may certainly find in the verbal texture of a play a measure of coherence that will give us aesthetic satisfaction as we read. . . . But we must not in the theatre expect or demand a rigid adherence to a formulated pattern, however strongly that may seem to emerge from a reading of the text.

No plays have seemed more closely organized around basic intellectual concepts than the 'last' plays or romances. Critics have varied in describing those concepts, but one and all 'read' the comedies as allegories. For F. C. Tinkler in *Scrutiny* (1937), the 'larger rhythm' of *The Winter's Tale* was the 'association between the ideas of a divine king and the rhythm of the seasons'. For F. D. Hoeniger, in *The University of Toronto Quarterly* (1950):

> Leontes' paradise at the end of the play is not, like Perdita's, that of a garden, but of a city and a temple, corresponding to the Heavenly City in the New Testament, the Temple of God. There he remarries Hermione, just as Dante meets Beatrice again, and Faust the eternal form of Gretchen.

Or Wilson Knight saw

> Leontes, under the tutelage of the Oracle, as painfully working himself from the bondage of sin and remorse into the freedom of nature, with the aptly-named Paulina as conscience, guide and priestess.

Yet *how* are these ideas expressed in the *plays*? In surveying the criticism of *The Winter's Tale* and other romances from 1900 to 1957 in a retrospective article in *Shakespeare Survey*, XI (1958), Philip Edwards argues that to discern the pattern was often to lose the play: the question that still obstinately remained was 'what are these plays like?' He concludes his article unsatisfied:

> To criticize the last plays in terms of the formal requirements of romance and the emotional response of the audience seems to me a very strenuous task considering the temptations we are exposed to of taking short cuts to Shakespeare's vision.

All three critics are suspicious of the pursuit of 'meaning', and Professor Edwards calls for a new 'modest' beginning.

What a play does must be the object of our research, and what it does in performance in a theatre: the 'felt impression', the 'mood', the experience of an audience, the 'requirements of romance and the emotional response of an audience'.

Here, I think, are the new concerns of Shakespeare studies today; and we must expect to remain in uncertainties, mysteries, doubts, to be modest and strenuous.

Much earlier in this century there had been an attempt at theatrical criticism: R. G. Moulton's *Shakespeare as a Dramatic Artist* led the way in 1885, and he was followed by G. P. Baker's *Development of Shakespeare as a Dramatist* (1907), Brander Matthews's *Shakespeare as a Playwright* (1913) and Muriel Bradbrook's *Elizabethan Stage Conditions: a Study of their Place in the Interpretation of Shakespeare's Plays* (1932). But the line died out, partly because these studies served the dominant concerns of character analysis, development or interpretation, partly for lack of terms comparable with those of more literary studies, and partly because the critics read the texts too often, to the exclusion of seeing the plays in performance. Only Granville-Barker, who knew the plays at first-hand as a theatre director, was able to write studies that have been in constant use up to today and are able to help the new movement back to a consideration of the plays in performance.

For now the task is being taken up afresh. Una Ellis–Fermor's posthumous and incomplete *Shakespeare the Dramatist* (1961) echoes the titles of the first decades of this century, but it is more radical and tentative: there are chapters on 'The Dramatic Mode', 'The Function of Plot' and, most significantly, on the 'secret impressions' in *Coriolanus*—those elements which are communicated by silences and without textual explicitness. This last chapter has attracted most attention from reviewers and suggests that Professor Ellis–Fermor was moving from an ambitious scheme for a general book on dramaturgy to a collection of detailed discoveries, from a consideration of strategy to reports from a hard-fought engagement.

Betrand Evans's *Shakespeare's Comedies* (1960) is also more detailed than its title suggests; he has taken one aspect of a play in performance—the moments when the audience knows more or less than the characters, or when one character knows more than others on stage, and so on—and uses this practical consideration as an approach to the plays. The book is one-sided and narrow, and while one reviewer praised it as the 'best' on Shakespeare's plays *as plays* in the last decade, I doubt if that reviewer had read it all. It is exhaustive, but also exhausting; the author clutches his card index:

> The seventeen comedies and romances included 297 scenes, in 170 of which an arrangement of descrepant awarenesses is the indespensable condition of dramatic effect. . . . Further, the comedies include 277 names persons . . . of whom 151 stand occasionally, frequently, or steadily in a condition of exploitable ignorance.

There is no concern with 'meaning' here, only a painstaking attempt to be precise and complete in considering one aspect of a play in performance.

In this, Evans is one among a growing number who are testing new ways of approach. B. L. Joseph has published chapters from a book on Elizabethan attitudes to performances. Muriel Bradbrook has deserted more literary studies of the structure of comedies, or a comparison of Shakespeare with other Elizabethan poets, to document *The Rise of the Common Player* (1962). Professor A. C. Sprague has used stage-history—the achievements of various actors and directors—to explore the theatrical possibilities of *Shakespeare's Histories* (1964). Anne Righter has written *Shakespeare and the Idea of the Play* (1962) which attempts a description of various modes of dramatic illusion. The Annual Shakespeare Association Lecture for 1962 by Richard David was called *Shakespeare and the Actors*. Nevill Coghill has discussed *Shakespeare's Professional Skills* (1964) in a book that draws upon his own experiences as a theatre director and sees Shakespeare as a theatrical craftsman. In *The Masks of Othello* (1961) Marvin Rosenberg has examined specific interpretations by actors of Shakespeare's characters, not because any of them give complete, or even completely faithful accounts, but because they all had to be maintained in performance, before an audience—they are indications of how the play works. Jan Kott's *Shakespeare, Our Contemporary,* originally published in Polish in 1961, recorded his own, highly individual, plans for directing some of the plays in the theatre as he knows it today.

The renewed study of Shakespeare's plays in performance comes at a time when the theatre itself is very concerned with its own possibilities. As Mondrian or Matisse, in very different ways, simplified their artistic means to line and colour in order to explore new kinds of painting, so dramatists like Ionesco or Beckett have become concerned with their techniques and have eliminated some obvious means as plot or narrative in order to concentrate on others that are peculiar to the theatre. Authors have turned towards the drama as an opportunity for expressing a commitment or an awareness in something like its human, as opposed to literary, complexity. Here is Harold Pinter on his own work:

> I am not a theorist. I'm not an authoritative or reliable commentator on the dramatic scene, the social scene, any scene. I write plays, when I can manage it, and that's all. That's the sum of it. . . . [I speak about my work] with some reluctance, knowing that there are at least twenty-four possible aspects of any single statement, depending on where you're standing at the time or on what the weather's like. A categorical statement, I find, will never stay where it is and be finite. (*Sunday Times,* 4 March 1962)

Something of this complexity, and of a desire to discover, is mirrored in our modern theatre, and also in the new Shakespeare studies. We do not seek a 'meaning'; we work towards a fuller, more responsible 'involvement'. We are more modest, more rigorous, and more varied in method and mood, than critics of previous decades.

I have spoken chiefly of critical studies of Shakespeare, rather than technical ones. This is because technical procedures are less susceptible to change. Research is a continuing, accommodating enterprise; we *always* can use more facts, or define the nature of evidence more precisely. In the study of Shakespeare's texts, his language, his sources, and of the Elizabethan theatre, the last decades have seen unprecendented advances: this is undisputed. And so the critics of today will be able to make fewer mistakes: they will be more precise where precision is possible, even while they become less assured and more modest as they attempt to understand the artistic achievement of the plays themselves.

August 1966

SHAKESPEARE PRODUCTION TODAY*

John Russell Brown

Everything I can say about Shakespeare's plays in performance today will be wrong. No one statement will cover every
play, or every moment of any one play, or all the various
ways in which Shakespeare is produced on the stages of the
world—in Canada, Ceylon, China and Czechoslovakia, in
India, Israel, Italy and Japan. I can speak best for the theatres
of Great Britain, and for the performances I have seen there
or in other European countries; but from this limited experience I am sure that I will never be unequivocally right.

Except in saying that I will never be right. And perhaps
this realization is the special mark of the production of
Shakespeare in our theatres today. The Victorial actor-
director, Henry Irving, spent his long career mounting
large-scale productions of numerous plays, convinced that
he was proceeding in the right way; if one production was
less successful than another, the fault was either the play's
or, possibly, the leading actor's in failing to adapt to the
demands of the particular role. Irving absorbed a few new
influences readily, but that was made the easier because the
general strategy of his productions—the formation of his
company, his use of scenery and music, his style of acting—
all remained unchanged. A century earlier David Garrick
had directed Shakespeare at Drury Lane for some thirty
years with basic assumptions that were never challenged;

* An earlier version of this lecture was published in *Divadlo* (Prague
1965), pp. 49–53.

he came to accept more elaborate spectacle—new scenery for each new play he directed, for instance—but always with some unwillingness. Or, again, Kemble's productions— statuesque compositions with supernumeraries organized around a dominant, simply-conceived hero—were not only consistent in his own time, but also in the work of his successors. So, for the eighteenth and nineteenth centuries, Shakespeare was a 'classic' in the sense that his plays were accepted in accepted ways; every thirty or fifty years there were changes, but these were modifications to established procedures, generally accepted movements in a single direction to accommodate production methods to the particular spirit of each age.

Today, in some countries Shakespeare is still a classic in this sense: in Paris, Jean-Louis Barrault's production of *Hamlet* first seen in 1948 was still being performed, unchanged in essentials, in the nineteen-sixties. This director has defined his attitude to such a play in *The Theatre of Jean-Louis Barrault* (1959):

> A classical play which has been tested by time should be more readily accepted by the public than a new play. The public knows what to expect and if the new production succeeds in reconciling tradition with freshness there is every chance that the public will find in it pleasure and profit. . . . I should be ashamed to have a flop with a classic!

This used to be our attitude to Shakespeare: we knew what to do, we knew it would 'work' and we blamed ourselves if we failed. But today, in Great Britain at any rate, we know we fail; we wonder sometimes if we can ever succeed.

In 1963, the Directors of the Royal Shakespeare Theatre collaborated on a pamphlet about the aims of their company, calling it *Crucial Years*:

Let our motto be: 'Keep open, keep critical' [wrote Peter Hall]. . . . Our Company is young. We are searching, and whatever we find today, a new search will be necessary tomorrow. The theatre is a quest, not an acceptance.

In our theatres, in contrast to earlier ones, directors are almost proud to fail with a classic; or are determined to demand the right to fail. In 1964 the production of *Hamlet* at Stratford, Connecticut, suffered last-minute resignations; and a few years before this company had sought a new chief director after a crop of acknowledged failures and resignations. In 1966 the new director resigned and yet another had to be found. This is nothing to be surprised about: it is the way of our theatres. The Royal Shakespeare Company in England has recently had great popular successes with productions of *King Lear* and the history plays, but in 1963 it had resounding failures with well-tried plays like *Julius Caesar* and *The Tempest,* and in 1964, the quartercentenary year, it mounted a fantastic *Merry Wives of Windsor,* with Alice-in-Wonderland costumes and plenty of musical bounce, that met a stony reception from the critics. The *Julius Caesar* was particularly thorough in flouting tradition; an open, bare, towering set with long entrances that dwarfed the actors for the important soliloquies and for the intensities of the great quarrel scene; drab colours and sackcloth texture replaced the usual Roman wealth and dignity; actors were cast for rhetorically demanding parts who had never before sustained a large Shakespearian role. Yet, after a cold first night, the play continued in the repertory, never rigorously reproduced: it was a particular attempt, a wrong turning in the new quest; and it was presented as such: 'Come and see our interesting failure.' In its last season before giving place to the new National Theatre, the Old Vic Company in London had two considerable failures, an *Othello* and a *Merchant of Venice.*

Neither in England nor America will it seem strange to say that every statement about directing Shakespeare in our theatres is bound to be inadequate—partly wrong. Some directors seem to be consciously looking for new ways of being wrong, even for unacceptable ways of directing a play that may in some future time be successful. An account of Peter Brook directing *King Lear* at Stratford-upon-Avon, published in the *Tulane Drama Review* (1964) tells how

> With the first night performance six hours away, the company was asked to give an easy, underplayed rendering of the play so to conserve their energies for the evening performance. Actors who had been belting out the verse since the first readings were suddenly giving scaled-down, unfussingly true performances. Basic relationships, so long obscured during erratic rehearsals, suddenly became crystal clear. . . . Those performances which were organically rooted and internally-based were revealed in a bright, non-shakespearian clarity. . . . Brook was hypnotized by the effect. 'You see how little you really need in order to capture the reality. If only theatre audiences listened to plays with the same intensity as concert audiences listen to Oistrakh, the performance of a play would be so much richer. . . . You see this level of acting,' he pointed to the stage where modern-dress actors were moving easily through the Hovel Scene, 'in thirty years this is the way all Shakespeare will be played'.

As in other forms of 'modern' art—most obviously in painting and musical composition—the door to Shakespeare production seems to have been kicked wide open to admit almost anything in the name of experiment, to welcome the charlatan. But like other statements about Shakespeare, this is partly untrue. First—as in painting or music—bad workmanship soon becomes obvious and almost as soon condemned. But second, and perhaps more important, the need to do well in a new way *more than once*—that is to go on being experimental—induces responsibility and a deepening knowledge of Shakespeare. On the one hand new experimentation is a free-for-all, but on the other it may bring about a renewed meeting with Shakespeare's plays themselves, by-passing accepted notions on order to respond originally to his colossal and imaginative creations—and if *that* is achieved by our experimenting directors, then, in time, the 'crucial years' may well become significant years. In fact the impression of unrestricted freedom is false. Everything that is said about Shakespeare's plays in performance is not only partly wrong, but carries along with it a recognition of its opposite. Today's directors may try to be true primitives and initiate simply, but the day is too late, too much experience has already been assimilated; one experiment is affected by many others.

Here then is cause for optimism about our theatres: Shakespeare producers work at a time when experimentation is welcomed, when everything said about their task is known to be wrong as well as right. Trivialities may be accepted for a time, but bad workmanship is soon evident, and scepticism and pragmatism may be leading some directors more deeply and more widely into Shakespeare's created world.

Only by paradoxes can the size and opportunities of the producer's task today be adequately expressed. This can be shown for example, by considering the obvious and often-repeated axiom, that Shakespeare wrote a poetic drama. Professor Knights, whom I quoted yesterday, has argued that the verbal life of the plays is the heart of Shakespeare's creation, rather than 'the more easily extractable elements of "plot" and "character"'. Peter Hall, in an interview to the London *Times* in the year he became Director of the Stratford-upon-Avon company, applied such a notion to his own tasks:

Shakespeare is not a dramatist of understatement. What he says, what he literally means and what he emotionally means, is fully expressed in his writing as if it were a piece of music.

These opinions have had important consequences in Shakespeare production. Not only is there a renewed interest in 'verse-speaking' after years of suspicion, but an increasing tendency to frame or isolate the longer and more obviously poetic speeches. In reviving his production of *A Midsummer Night's Dream* (1959) in a later season, Peter Hall restored some speeches earlier cut for lack of plot-interest and gave the fairies two modes of speaking, a natural one and another, specially studied one for poetic passages. Such are limited responses to this facet of Shakespeare's dramaturgy. But a director can also learn to rely on the verbal complexity of the plays for inducing atmosphere or mood, for controlling tempo, presenting an unspecified yet important aspect of a particular character, emphasizing certain abstract themes or implied locations. When, after the death of Hector, Achilles says:

> The dragon wing of night o'erspreads the earth
> And, stickler-like, the armies separates,

his words contribute to the narrative and to placing the incident that has just occurred, but they also achieve much else beside. 'Stickler-like', a nonce word for Shakespeare, relates war to a tournament and to a partisan and, perhaps, fictitious quarrel; and its syntactical and metrical position, causing the iambic pentameter to hesitate near its beginning, gives a pedantic, considered or even fussy tone to the line in contrast to the long-paced inevitability of the preceding line. The two pentameters, together, give enormous scale and unchallenged power to night and to natural processes and also belittle the activity of the dramatis personae. The next two lines, with short phrases and simple, directly physical images, again in contrast with the preceding lines, mark Achilles' motives as unquestioned, physical and satisfied:

> My half-supp'd sword, that frankly would have fed,
> Pleas'd with this dainty bait, thus goes to bed.

And, of course, the themes of the play—time, heroism, judgement and appetite, fate—are all reflected in this passage.

For these and many other reasons we must say that Shakespeare's drama is poetic and the spoken word of central importance, and that a production must take care of the text. But at once this must be qualified: words are not always important; much lies behind the words, between the lines; what is not said is often more important than any spoken word. There are obvious moments when stage action takes over from speech. At the end of Volumnia's pleading, Coriolanus expresses his last-minute reliance on instinct rather than will by a simple movement indicated by the stage-direction: '*He holds her by the hand, silent.*' In *Hamlet*, the prince's silent entry in black contributes to the dramatic effect of the first court scene long before he speaks: the good Quarto edition of 1604/5 directs that, after the King and Queen, the Councillors, Polonius and Laertes, Hamlet should enter '*cum aliis*', not like the hero of the piece, but like a Prufrock, 'an attendant lord'; the star actor in this play starts silently in notable eclipse, an image of a disordered state and strained affections. Later, in Act IV Scene v, the almost silent figures of Gertrude, Claudius and Horatio contrast with the volubility and incessant movement of the mad Ophelia; they say just enough to show that they cannot communicate with her and to draw attention to their helpless and mostly tongue-tied presence. In the following scene, the unspecified number of sailors from the pirate ship who enter to Horatio will, by their dress and bearing, represent the strange world—uncouth and uncommunicative in comparison with Elsinore—in which Hamlet has become able to act with resolution and rapidity; Horatio will probably look at them as he reads Hamlet's description of 'these good fellows' and so draw new attention to the now silent messengers, alien, and uncertain where to go in Elsinore. Sometimes a stage-property speaks more than words: the coffin of Ophelia during the slow funeral entry; or the bloody head of Macbeth which is all the audience can gaze at to satisfy its need to know how he had died.

The importance of what a character expresses underneath or against his words is more difficult to establish, because a more pervasive influence. Shakespeare's fondness for disguise is perhaps the most obvious clue: so Rosalind can verbally 'misuse her sex' in *As You Like It* and yet show by sudden transitions of mood, sudden deflexions from the apparent subject-matter, by strange silences or willful exaggerations, how her physical and emotional reactions are nearly all the time tugging away from the line of her spoken thoughts. There are disguises in history plays and tragedies too: the murder-planning Macbeth is the reality under his words to Duncan that speak only of loyalty and trust; the fearful Macbeth holds the brave and active soldier silent while Banquo is left to interrogate the witches—here the almost silent figure is obviously the centre and motor-element of the scene rather than the reasonable talker—and when Macbeth's soliloquy at last comes, it shows that his earlier, modest speech to Banquo about the witches was a cloak and not an expression of his reactions. So, under the confident words of Richard III in the first half of the play, the actor must impress some hints of the later Richard, the one who 'gnaws his lip', who has 'deep enemies' to his rest and whose last resource is not his boasted subtlety but a blind and angry courage. The actor has far more to do than express Shakespeare's meaning fully in words, as if they were a musical or total expression.

In many plays verbal disguise is a constant element of the dramatic interest, words often misrepresenting a speaker's response to situation and action; feelings, instincts, thoughts and affections may lie under the surface of speech, sometimes purposely and often unconsciously. In his first sustained speech Hamlet acknowledges something 'within' that passes 'show'; his words may be 'windy suspiration of forc'd breath', only 'forms' of grief that can never 'denote' him 'truly'. If his first soliloquy is examined for its ostensible meaning, for what it 'explicitly says', Hamlet would seem to be motivated above all by repugnance at his mother's new marriage, and his mind fixed upon 'things rank and gross in nature'; but, if we look for what is *not* said, only hinted at, or approached and then avoided, we may see that Hamlet is drawn chiefly to his father and to truth and nobility, a kind of purity. Already, in the earlier speech he had been concerned with being denoted 'truly'. Now, dissatisfied with his 'too, too solid flesh' (or 'sallied', or 'sullied'; the ambiguity of this word, like the repeated 'too', suggests a pressure of feeling and thought not easily defined or fixed), he dwells more patiently on 'melt', 'thaw', 'resolve' and 'dew' (and here there may be a favourite Shakespeare pun on 'due'; the idea is picked up in the following 'fix'd' and 'canon'). Yet Hamlet's struggle with words stops abruptly with 'That it should come to this!'; in reading we may think that 'this' refers to the 'unweeded garden', but the actor has to move from 'this' to 'But two months dead!'; and he can only effect this transition with an impression of actuality if, between the two lines, Hamlet has thought of his father and, also, decided not to speak directly, even to himself, of this man. Only after contradictions of fact—'Nay, not so much, not two'—which break the flow of the iambic pentameter and change from coherent and even elaborate sentence-structure to ejaculation, is he ready to speak of his father—though not yet as his father:

> So excellent a king that was to this
> Hyperion to a satyr; so loving to my mother,
> That he might not beteem the winds of heaven
> Visit her face too roughly.

Here there is also an elaborate and considered gentleness, physical yet hardly real; an actual person has been transformed into an airiness, fantasy, spirituality. In the remainder of the soliloquy, Hamlet stops several times to shy away from his own thoughts: 'Heaven and earth! Must I remember?', 'Let me not think on't.' He now speaks of 'my poor father's body', but in connection with his mother or uncle, not with himself alone. He knows he must 'hold' his tongue but, when he is with Horatio and so has someone with whom to share his anger at his mother, that anger is stilled by a quite sudden ejaculation, 'My father', which has to be explained, 'methinks I see my father'. Hamlet is not so repelled by the world and his mother as he says or, perhaps, as he thinks; rather he is impelled by thoughts of his father, or of an almost mythical, spiritual, ideal king. He needs to be pure and inviolate. He expects his mother to be so, and when, after the closet scene, he believes that she is, he leaves her. He dies concerned for his 'wounded name' and accepting a future (or perhaps a new peace, for 'rest' might imply both) in 'silence'. Beneath Hamlet's words of apathy is an internal committal and activity, and beneath his dispersed and contradictory talk of his mother, his uncle, the state and himself, a concern with his own purity that can only be satisfied in his death.

Everything we say about Shakespeare in performance is

right *and* wrong: he wrote a poetic drama, fully expressed verbally; but the words are not all, for silence and gesture are also important, and the text often and importantly lies. The director must look for the purely visual dramatic expression and must sometimes encourage his actors to act against the apparent meaning of his words.

Paradoxes are also found in general matters, as in the composition of a company to present the plays. Certainly the actors should be a group, capable of ensemble-playing. The Chamberlain's and King's Men, Shakespeare's own company, were such; and the plays themselves often demand group effects. The close of *Henry IV*, Part 1 is general, sustained verbally by both Hal and the King but relying for its full effect on the three-line contribution of Worcester and the silent one of Vernon, who alone represent directly the cost of Henry's victory and of his usurpation of the crown. Moreover, the scene has to continue the interest of the audience who have just seen their favourite, Falstaff, leave the stage in a superbly climactic episode that blends seriousness and irresponsibility. The last moments of *Henry IV*, Part 2 are carried by neither king nor comic, but by two comparatively minor figures, the Lord Chief Justice and Prince John; if the company cannot cast these parts well, with actors expert at following the more obvious stars, the play will end with an unwanted anti-climax. Perhaps *Coriolanus* is most remarkable in this respect, for there the hero's death is largely defined by the action and cries of a large crowd of supers, and three anonymous lords share with Aufidius the final verbal judgement. The scenes with conspirators in *Julius Caesar,* especially the approach to the capital (III, i), show how Shakespeare expected his actors to control complicated activity across a crowded stage in such a way that one-line, or half-line, contributions can contribute exposition, surprise, suspense, suspicion or ominous threats.

75

The early comedies need a consistent style and superb team-work and timing; only so can *The Taming of the Shrew* move nimbly enough and its broad humour be sharpened to reveal wit and Shakespeare's psychological and social understanding. (A production of this play by the Company of Four in Milan in 1962 was an eloquent criticism of the heavy and individually pointed performances of English productions that so often cripple the play.)

But as a Shakespearian company needs group training and a permanent establishment, so it also needs the apparent opposite—individual star actors. Shakespeare wrote for stars: Richard Burbage, the chief actor of his company, was said never to leave the stage without applause—a response more usual in opera houses than Shakespearian theatres in England or America today. The tragedies and histories alike have dominating roles, often in contrast to the source material from which Shakespeare worked. Certain tasks could only be attempted by actors trained to centre attention on themselves, to sustain an individual rhythm so that they can make a strong impression by economical means—Coriolanus responding to Volumnia's stream of rhetoric with a hand movement is a case in point, if the gesture is to seem heroic enough for the large setting of the Volscian army ready to burn Rome. The middle passages of *King Lear,* on the heath and on Dover Beach, have negligible plot-development, confusing action and often baffling words; and so the audience's attention must be held by the star actor's power to shape the words and actions with which Shakespeare has explored the welling-up of subconscious love and hatred. Actors who play the tragic heroes must also be capable of astonishing concentration, as at the end of *Hamlet* where 'The point envenom'd too! Then, venom, to thy work' must sum up all the moral issues inconclusively explored earlier in long soliloquies and elaborate action; and 'the rest is silence' must seem a true conclusion. Shakespeare wrote in confident expectation that star actors would be found to sustain, control and illuminate the star roles; his plays will often fall flat without such help—as they will also go lamely and confusedly without ensemble-playing.

When considering the task of producing Shakespeare in our theatres today, paradox may be piled on paradox. The setting should represent the form of an Elizabethan theatre; yet it should also help adapt the play to new theatre buildings and new visual habits of the audiences. Lighting should not attract attention to itself nor limit the basically large stage space; but it can and, I think, should help to intensify certain moments and be used to suggest the various settings of the scenes with the rapidity and economy called for by Shakespeare's narrative methods. If we now need more actualization of location, lighting may be the best means of getting sufficient variety and sufficient speed of change. Directors need a firm control of their actors to give shape to the more elaborate scenes and to emphasize the analogical structure of the plays, the thematic connections between plot and subplot; but they should also give actors the freedom necessary for investigating the subtextual life of their roles because only so will the actors bring the deepest resources of their individual imagination and beings to the climactic revelations of character which provide dominant effects in every one of Shakespeare's plays.

Productions need to be fantastic, easily encompassing the Forest of Arden, fairies, spirits and 'quaint devices'; presenting gods, witches, good spirits and bad, disguises of both appearance and nature, statues that come alive, an old enchantress, a timely gravedigger who began digging graves the day Hamlet was born and digs up Yorick's skull as unknowingly he speaks to Hamlet; and productions also need to be realistic, showing the modern psychological and social truth,

77

contemporary as well as Elizabethan, in the motivation and behaviour of Richard III or Malvolio, or Othello, the every-day day-dream world in Illyria or Arden, everyman's responsibility in Prospero's astonishing, renaissance craft, or everyman's need of a 'good heart' in the successes, cruelties and embarrassments of Henry V.

Theatre directors should be both conservative *and* radically experimental. Conservative because not to learn from what has gone before is to involve oneself in unnecessary muddle and mistakes. *Twelfth Night* can be overweighted on its comic side: reviews warn producers that Viola and Olivia can be submerged in the roistering Belch and Aguecheek and some versions of Malvolio. Autolycus in *The Winter's Tale* needs a self-sufficient comic to elaborate the moments provided for him by Shakespeare: it is one of Shakespeare's least scripted parts and actors unused to comic by-play have failed in the role again and again. Falstaff, on the other hand, is seldom a success when played by a 'comic': Garrick or Ralph Richardson have succeeded where Yates, or Shuter, or George Robey have failed. *Macbeth* has a tendency to fall off towards the end; a great reserve of strength is needed for the enactment of the last scenes, for the rapid transitions of mood and for the last fight; yet time and again the actor has not sufficiently husbanded his resources. In Shakespeare production it pays to be conservative, to learn from the experience of earlier actors and directors. And yet the opposite is also true: it pays to be adventurous, experimental and impudent. The history of Shakespeare in the theatre is a series of revelations, or surprises. Macklin's realistic Shylock in place of a broadly comic one evoked the astonished doggerel:

This is the Jew
That Shakespeare drew.

Granville-Barker's elegant and stylish production of *A Midsummer Night's Dream*, in place of a thickly detailed attempt to creat a 'true English' forest scene, rediscovered the elegance and wit of the play—even if the mechanicals and Bottom missed out. The Stratford-upon-Avon production of the history plays in 1964 revealed many opportunities that Shakespeare has provided for showing the suffering and loss of war, and also Shakespeare's ruthless political satire in the earlier plays. Constantly newspaper critics speak of 'revelation' and often they are hailing something of trivial importance; but the paradox remains, Shakespeare in our theatres must be not only conservative but also boldly innovating; without the innovation we may never stumble on some parts of the hidden treasure.

Everything we say about Shakespeare must be wrong. Today when this becomes increasingly recognized, we stand in a position where experimentation is possible, accepted and necessary. Many individual talents and the cultures of many nations and races are brought freely to bear on the problems of producing Shakespeare in our theatres. If we are watchful and responsible, as well as imaginative and daring—even impudent—we may come closer than before to showing, in the mirror Shakespeare held up to nature, the feature of virtue and image of scorn, and find a way of presenting the form and pressure of the very age and body of our own time. But, again, here is a paradox, for the new freedom may also permit us to indulge trivial notions and so depart further than ever before from a real presentation of Shakespeare's image of our world.

I started by saying that everything we say about Shakespeare's plays in performance must be partly wrong, and that this realization is the special mark of our productions today. From this derives a new need for responsible criticism and I want to end by emphasizing this. With more freedom to experiment should come a consequently greater consideration. Granted the pre-eminent achievement of Shakespeare—which was internationally attested in the quartercentennial celebrations of his birth—we are justified in asking for extraordinary pains to be taken. I believe that new, concerted study should be the next step in our changing approach to Shakespeare production.

For scientists, experimentation naturally implies co-operation and meticulous sifting of evidence; no scientist today can work alone. (The few spectacular and terrible rivalries between nations in research only accentuate the usual spirit of co-operation that is a mark of scientific experimentation.) And so we should work in the new era of experimental Shakespeare production.

Such a plea may sound too complicated and pedestrian for an artistic task, but that objection is answered with another paradox—that individual creativity should also be sought to the highest degree. And it must not be allowed to obscure the obvious need: the simple fact is that in England and the United States at least, experimentation is easy and responsibility unnecessarily difficult. In our busy and profitable theatres there is insufficient time to think and compare; and in our struggling and improvised theatres there is insufficient co-operation between one company and another, or between directors and scholars. There is no multilingual or English-language periodical devoted to the problems of Shakespeare production.

The separation of scholarship and practice is absurd at a time when our theatre directors are urging their companies to 'keep open, keep critical', and vowing that they 'are searching; . . . the theatre is a quest, not an acceptance.' At the large and generously sponsored International Shakespeare Conference at Stratford-upon-Avon designed to mark the

400th anniversary of Shakespeare's birth, not one English or American director, actor or scene designer was present.

The books published each year about Shakespeare indicate the same lack of critical work in our theatres. Since 1947, when the last of Granville-Barker's *Prefaces* was published, no English or American director has found the time and interest to write in useful detail about his work; and no scholarly, or indeed popular, writer about Shakespeare has also been widely accepted as a professional theatre director. The most that can be shown are some reviews of current productions written each year by scholars to which theatre people pay little regard, and some interviews, programme notes, short essays or talks to actors that have been published by directors, usually in ephemeral form. The wide interest taken in the book of Polish man of the theatre, Jan Kott's *Shakespeare, Our Contemporary*—a book ill-formed, unbalanced and, I am told, badly translated—shows that both theatre directors and scholars can be reached by a single piece of criticism.

Nothing that we say about producing Shakespeare in our theatres today can be wholly right; the theatre is accepting experimentation as the new basis of its productions; there is a new need for responsible, historically informed and nevertheless practical, theatrical criticism: this as I see it is the present condition of Shakespeare production, that phenomenon that has had a pre-eminent place for more than three hundred years in English-speaking theatres and, increasingly in recent years, in the theatres throughout the world.

August 1966

SECOND CENTURY SHAKESPEARE

Herbert Whittaker

For our distinguished visitors, I must quickly explain that I am not offering another sample of North American scholarship which purports to prove that Shakespeare was not an Elizabethan English playwright but the accumulation of writers dating back to some other Homer in 200 A.D. The 'Second Century' of my title refers to the second century of Confederation which Canada is just about to enter. Thus my talk is not an excursion into the past of William Shakespeare but a speculation about his future here in Canada.

In 1964, the year of Shakespeare's quadricentenary, I took advantage of this forum presented by the Stratford Seminars to remind Canadians that Shakespeare was not imported to this country by Sir Tyrone Guthrie in 1953—like so much Irish jam. Importing culture is one thing we didn't have to wait for Tyrone Guthrie to teach us. We have a tradition of importing what we need, including the essence of other people's civilizations, which goes back to our earliest beginnings.

Our importation of Shakespeare in his printed form probably began soon after the Folios were available. The Bible and Shakespeare were traditionally part of the civilized explorer's kit. For the performance of Shakespeare we had to wait until the American Revolution drove our first cry of Shakespearians up from Albany.

But I do not propose to review once again that touching comic history of the acting of Shakespeare's plays in this country. When I did it roughly three years ago, I attempted to show how all the conditions which made this Stratford Festival a success had been available in Canada before 1953 but only when all the right ingredients were combined under the right conditions by the right people did Canada produce this theatre, now a principal ornament of its culture.

That earlier talk led me to the threshold of the Stratford Festival Theatre. Now I would like to pursue the topic of Shakespeare in Canada along a path that will review the accomplishments of this theatre briefly and permit me to indulge in some speculation about the future of Stratford, and Shakespeare, in Canada in the second century of our Confederation.

'July 14, 1953, was the most exciting night in the history of Canadian theatre. I doubt if there will ever be another night to match it, for me and for a great many others who were at that opening of the first Stratford Festival. . . . No glories since can dim our recollection of the night when the cannon first startled us, the bell hushed us into expectancy and the lights came up on the figure of Alec Guinness, astride the parapet in the guise of Richard III.' That rather emotional recollection—a quotation from a not very popular book I wrote about the Festival's earliest years—sounds faraway and naive today. It has the possessiveness that pioneers impose on their descendants—as to say: 'Ah, had you but known it all then!' In fact, I am not sure it doesn't remind me of a distinguished critical colleague of my earliest days, S. Morgan-Powell of Montreal, who announced that I would never see Hamlet if I had not seen Sir Johnston Forbes-Robertson's noble impersonation of the role. As Sir Johnston was regrettably dead by then, my senior officer was condemning me to a life of frustration in this matter of Hamlets. Perhaps it was the kind of pioneer's curse he put on me—but to this day I have never seen a Hamlet who left me as convinced as Forbes-Robertson had obviously convinced S. Morgan-Powell.

But that is digression. We need only to go back fourteen years for my purposes here. Tom Patterson and his associates had lured Tyrone Guthrie out to Canada to discuss the possibilities of some madcap scheme for putting on Shakespearian plays in the Ontario Stratford. We know the results so well that we take them for granted.

We don't stop to think what the idea presented, and what Tyrone Guthrie created, were very different in quality and scope. The hankering for the presentation of Shakespeare in Stratford, Ontario, was not even new with Tom Patterson though there had never been so staunch and ingenious an advocate for it. There is a bandstand that stands athwart the lake built many years ago to accommodate outdoor Shakespeare—which it never, as far as I know, did.

One proposal of the early committee was, I know, to have a bang-up Shakespeare Festival with a stage-coach running down Ontario Street. This I know first hand—because some Stratford businessmen dropped into the *Globe and Mail* office to see an old friend, Bruce West, and ask him his opinion of this young Patterson's hare-brained scheme. Mr. West kindly steered them over to me and thus started one of the happiest and most rewarding associations of my professional life: the chronicling of the growth and attainment of this Festival.

But Tom Patterson's committee had picked the right man, if not exactly the right ideas. And they picked the right man at the right time. Tyrone Guthrie had become a disciple of William Poel some years earlier in the latter's crusade to restore Shakespeare's plays to the kind of stage for which they were written, although he was not a purist in the matter as was Poel. But his productions at the Assembly Hall for Edinburgh's Festival had made him increasingly impatient of the proscenium as a container of the Bard. What Guthrie envisioned, and Tanya Moiseiwitsch created the image for, is the one you know, substantially unchanged. It is the mould which has shaped our Shakespeare in Canada—and in other parts of the world, too, we are proud to say.

The stage came first, as you know. Tanya Moiseiwitsch's arrangement of platforms, pillars, levels and fluted walls was tried out in a tent first. It was tried and found highly satisfactory for the playing of Shakespeare during the first four years of Stratford's existence. After that testing period, it was incorporated, with minimal changes to scale it to the new structure, into the building we now know and admire.

It is not often that a critic has the opportunity to point out his special appreciation of a stage while standing on it. I won't let this opportunity go to my head, and run about happily pointing out my favourite features. Instead I will content myself with emphasizing that the Stratford stage is a small stage, extended by the gutters and made more accessible by the vomitoriums, right and left, but still small in area. The backing allows the stage to be used vertically, as it were. The upper entrances permit the overlapping scenes—like dissolves in a film—which give such pace to Stratford productions when well used. The steps leading to the gutter permit the deploying of crowds while keeping leading performers in clear focus.

What this stage does not do is allow an actor to command the entire audience without turning his head. This is more, I suggest, a peculiarity of the auditorium than of the stage. Some actors deplore this more than others. Certainly Sir Laurence Olivier, reportedly one of the **few players** who did not fall head-over-heels in love with **this** Stratford stage, is insisting that there must be a point of command when his National Theatre of Great Britain builds its own variation on this Stratford stage beside the Thames.

While I am hinting at the peculiarities of this famous stage, I might do worse than repeat my story of that other noble English actor, Sir John Gielgud. Sir John was persuaded to launch his first *Ages of Man* tour in this theatre. His Canadian impresario called on me to suggest a town which might be included with Toronto on this tour and I suggested that while Stratford was not a big town it had a way of filling up for theatrical events of high quality. So Sir John took the Stratford stage.

He began his now-famous recital downstage centre, with the book beside him on a lectern—possibly this very one that I am using. But sensing his audience behind him, he gradually backed upstage to be able to encompass the full house. Speaking the words of Shakespeare more beautifully than they had ever been spoken here before, he nevertheless became aware that he had a rival on stage. It was the centre pillar, the magnetic pole of this great structure. Sir John dealt with his mute rival as only a great actor or a great politician could—he joined it, simply by putting his hand on it. Needless to say, all this adjustment to the Stratford stage was subconscious on Sir John's part, but it provided for the watchers a very entertaining illustration of what the actor must contend with when he stands on Stratford's stage.

That this stage is as tricky as Richard III and as stubborn as Katherine the Shrew is no secret. Its victims are part of Stratford's history, along with the successes of Sir Tyrone Guthrie and Tanya Moiseiwitsch. Perhaps you might even account its second director as one of them. Cecil Clarke came to Stratford as its assistant director and production manager in 1953 with the record of having been the youngest brigadier in the British army during the last war, and his special gifts stood Stratford in very good stead that first year. It was in the second year, 1954, that Mr. Clarke was entrusted with the responsibility of staging *Measure for Measure*, while Sir

Tyrone applied himself to *Oedipus Rex* and *The Taming of the Shrew*. The intractable nature of the Stratford stage showed itself for the first time. It was reported that Sir Tyrone had to step in to help with the final rehearsals. Whether he did or not, it is fair to say that *Measure for Measure* was not a great success, despite Frances Hyland's characterful Isabella and James Mason's dignity as Angelo.

Yet Cecil Clarke knew and appreciated this stage. In the very first programme, before the very first production, he had written:

> Whether this stage will ever achieve universal popularity and become, as it were, the blueprint for Shakespearean and perhaps other classical productions in the years to come, remains to be seen. Let us hope so; . . . it is really up to the audiences. If they can accept the new intimacy of this stage without embarrassment and feel that they can participate fully in performances, then this form of theatre will indeed progress and be able to offer enter-tainment which is, in every way, vital.

The audiences did accept Mr. Clarke's challenge and Stratford did provide a blue-print, as we know, for other productions, other stages, other theatres—and will for many more to come. It is worth remembering that Cecil Clarke foresaw this from the beginning.

There have been other victims of this Stratford stage—other directors and actors, too. Learning to act on this stage also takes patience and application (and I suspect a good deal of guesswork) until the audience arrives to tell you whether you were right or not, as my good friend Roberta Beatty of Montreal would say.

I don't think Lorne Greene, the best-known of all Canadian performers, would object to my saying that he was one of the actors who fell victim to the capricious Stratford stage. I remember driving back to Stratford from Toronto with him after he had made a not-too-successful debut as Brutus in *Julius Caesar* and his exclaiming, 'Why didn't somebody tell me how to act on that stage!' That was in the season of 1955, and the person who might have been expected to tell him was the new young director, Michael Langham, whom Tyrone Guthrie had brought in as co-director. Perhaps Mr. Greene could not be told, perhaps Mr. Langham didn't know what to tell him. Perhaps Mr. Langham didn't know then. Not all of that *Julius Caesar* was first-rate, as I remember, and Mr. Greene's was not its only disappointing performance, but in his handling of the Forum Scene and the death of Cinna the Poet, the new young successor to Cecil Clarke showed that he was a David with instincts for subduing such a giant as Stratford. The Forum Scene was particularly exciting, for Mr. Langham scattered his mob all through the tent, so that we all became part of that malleable gang of Romans. Some of us were tempted to shout a warning about Mark Antony's strategy, but restrained ourselves. In this day of 'happenings' in the theatre, would you change the ending of even your least-favourite Shakespearian play if offered the chance? Today, we rarely see an actor step off the stage here in Stratford. We are startled when Falstaff departs through the house this season in David William's production of *The Merry Wives*. In the old days, it seemed that the actors were as much off as on.

Tyrone Guthrie, who had evolved this stage, came to its first seasons with some already well-developed ideas as to how such an open stage should be used, many of them tested in Edinburgh's Festival Hall. The generous use of the aisles was part of his technique, and his alarums, sorties and sallies forth kept the early tent audiences in a great state of nervous excitement. Those were circus days. Banners and processions, other Guthrie trade-marks, filled the tent with movement. The acting was big and bold to match all, and Guthrie found a great trick of orchestration by which he was able to build the climaxes of his productions into tremendous operatic finales. His trial scene that same year, 1955, offered a case in point: never had the fate of Shylock seemed in so much doubt, I am convinced, since the very first production.

All was not smash and splash in Guthrie's productions, of course. The Belmont scene which followed that tremendous trial was as tender and lyrical a coda as could be desired. If Guthrie knew the value of noise and great action, he also knew the value of sharp contrast. He had set the standards for Canada's Stratford Festival Theatre even before it was built. His presence haunts every director who succeeds him here, just as the original choices of Tanya Moiseiwitsch affect every other designer who works for this stage. Their contributions are built into the very structure of Stratford and can no more be overlooked than they can be forgotten.

In addition to Cecil Clarke, a surprising number of directors have wrestled with this stage. The list of them is surprising—both in its length and in the fact that one is surprised at having forgotten so many vital contributors. Of course, some of them are far from forgotten: Douglas Campbell, for instance, a dynamic member of the first company who directed and starred in Festival productions before moving to the Tyrone Guthrie Theatre in Minneapolis. George McCowan made less of an impression, being associate director with first Langham and then Jean Gascon before directing his solo efforts: *Henry VIII, The Tempest* and *The Canvas Barricade*. Then there were Peter Wood, who did the *As You Like It* in 1959; Douglas Seale, who did the *King John* in 1960; Peter Coe, who did the 1962 *Macbeth*; Stuart Burge, who did the 1964 *Richard II* and the next year's *Henry IV,* Part 1, and Part 2, known to the Festival as *Falstaff.* Which brings us to this year's directors, David William, who did last season's *Twelfth Night* and this year's *Merry Wives of Windsor,* and Jean Gascon and John Hirsch, who are to replace Langham in the artistic directorship next season.

It would be, of course, impossible as well as discourteous, to attempt any proper estimate of Michael Langham's contribution to the Stratford Festival as Tyrone Guthrie's successor at this point, but those of us who have watched Mr. Langham grow into the rare director he now is take special pleasure in recognizing that he has become the sensitive and brilliant director for the open stage that he is today entirely through his work on this particular platform. It is not a case of saying that Stratford taught him all he knows—but rather that Stratford provided the best laboratory for his experiment in the new form of the twentieth-century stage. In a dozen years—he came in 1955—with only one year away, Michael Langham has taken the exciting heritage of the Great Innovator, Tyrone Guthrie, and worried about it, pushed it, attempted new techniques, discarded many of them, delved, explored and come up again with a way of handling plays and actors on the Stratford stage that is his own and unique.

As we saw with the 1955 *Julius Caesar,* his first attempt employed this stage much as Guthrie did if with perhaps less success with the individual actors. There is a legend, doubted because it is so unlikely, that the actors once rose in protest against the newcomer, probably because they could not bear the idea of a successor to the revered Guthrie. The loyalty of the Stratford company is notably high, as some of the interim directors have learned. That loyalty was transferred to Langham very soon after Guthrie's departure from the scene in 1956, in time for one of the company's most individual successes—the first *Henry V* with Christopher Plummer and a fine representation of the best French-speaking actors of Canada, including Gratien Gelinas and Jean Gascon.

It is Guthrie's special quality that he can create a Shakespearian out of the raw material to hand, wherever he finds himself. He made particular efforts to see that Canada's Stratford was a Canadian company in language and spirit. Michael Langham has a different view on the matter, seeing a Shakespearian company as an aggregation necessarily international. In fact, if you ask an actor whether he thinks that Michael Langham will eventually return to England, the flip answer may come: 'When did he ever leave it?'—and this without a modicum of rancour. Yet one does not forget that it was Michael Langham who gave the Festival its great bi-cultural *Henry V* back in 1956. It was a production that only could have been created here—and indeed one which had no special message for anywhere else. This was made obvious by the English reviewers when the production, and the Guthrie *Oedipus Rex,* were taken to Edinburgh.

It was Michael Langham, too, who took Canada's Stratford company to Chichester eight years later, with a very different reception. On that occasion, Michael Langham was very much the director of a Canadian company—going to show off its wares in a building for which it had already suggested the rough blue-print.

Following that first *Henry V,* the Langham mastery of his new craft developed through a *Hamlet,* which opened this theatre in 1957, a fine *Much Ado About Nothing*—both with Christopher Plummer as star actor—a *Romeo and Juliet* on his return from a sabbatical, a *Coriolanus,* with Paul Scofield, and also with Scofield, a truly glorious *Love's Labour's Lost.* It was in this production that one recognized how different the Langham style had become from that of Guthrie. It was a difference of scale, of subtlety and humour.

The Taming of the Shrew and *Cyrano de Bergerac* followed in 1962, and then another splendid Langham advance with

Troilus and Cressida, accompanied by a *Timon of Athens,* less impressive but destined to improve when taken abroad. And then that memorable *King Lear,* a high point for this theatre. A second *Henry V,* very different in mood from the first, and the 1966 experiment in a new work, *The Last of the Tsars,* brought Michael Langham to this season's hilarious *Government Inspector* and the remarkable *Antony and Cleopatra* which we witnessed on Monday night, a production which may grow from that opening to become one of his major achievements. Certainly, it demonstrated the invention and imagination which has characterized his conquest of this Festival stage. This production was Michael Langham's swan song as Stratford's artistic director, although it is most certainly hoped that he will be back again to create other guest productions for the Festival, as Sir Tyrone has. The men who have mastered this particular stage are too rare to lose.

Now how about their successors? How about the men who will succeed Mr. Langham and thus will carry Stratford into the second century of Confederation?

I have admired the work of Jean Gascon and John Hirsch quite extravagantly on occasion—the last time being Mr. Hirsch's handling of *Colours in the Dark* at the Avon, but I will not pretend that either of them has acquired the full mastery of the Stratford stage. I will not pretend it here because I don't believe they have and besides it is on record how I feel about their often remarkable contributions.

Mr. Jean Gascon co-directed with George McCowan the *Othello* in 1959 and directed *The Comedy of Errors* in 1963 and *The Bourgeois Gentleman* in 1964. It is difficult to assess the first, although Mr. McCowan himself once remarked that it was Mr. Gascon who took the leading part in their collaboration. *The Comedy of Errors* suffered from Gallic impatience, for the director couldn't wait to show us his *commedia dell' arte* techniques and so never bothered to lay down the groundwork for his farce. *The Bourgeois Gentleman* found him on safer ground—for he had made his considerable reputation directing Molière for Montreal's Théâtre du Nouveau Monde. But Jean Gascon has enhanced the Stratford part of his reputation as its director of opera. He has displayed an extraordinary gift for this, and for this alone he would be worthy of the high trust Stratford is now putting in him. But there is still the matter of handling this stage, a mystery central to the Festival's very being.

Mr. Hirsch presents a somewhat different case. This production of *Colours in the Dark*, which impressed me as his best work for Stratford, was done at the Avon Theatre. Previous to that his best work for Stratford was probably the *Henry VI,* done in 1966, in which he took that blunt succession of melodramatic scenes and welded them together into a picture of period power politics. It was work more than workmanlike and promised well for this year's *Richard III*. On opening night that play proved a disappointment— with its ideas imposed on Shakespeare's rather than being part of them. It left Alan Bates in a very difficult position as Richard, or rather in a series of difficult positions. (One needs in fairness to add that the production has grown enormously during the season.)

Hirsch's introduction to the Festival, after he had established himself for his great pioneer work at the Manitoba Theatre Centre in Winnipeg, was the 1965 production of *The Cherry Orchard*. Much of this was loving and effective, but it did not counteract entirely the impression that the elusive Chekhov doesn't fit comfortably onto a stage as presentational as this one.

Which brings us to our major speculation as to the future of Stratford. With most of the Folio already staged, it is reasonable to think that Mr. Gascon and Mr. Hirsch will start to branch out more into other literary fields. Neither is totally committed as a Shakespearian director. Also, they can point out that the repetitions at Stratford hardly ever top the original productions—with the exception of Michael Langham's revival of *The Taming of the Shrew*.

But the Stratford stage has so far stubbornly reminded us that it was built for Shakespeare and that Sophocles, Chekhov, Rostand and Wycherley all turn awkward when forced onto its surface.

This is not to say that other classic dramatists would not suit the stage better. Euripedes rather than Sophocles, perhaps, and Ben Jonson rather than Congreve. And there is every reason to think that Brecht could suit this auditorium and this stage very well.

The alternative is to create new works for this stage, and this I think the Festival must come to. It made one unsuccessful attempt at this back in 1961. Then my paper, the *Globe and Mail,* held a competition for a new play, the winner to be actually staged here. Donald Jack's *The Canvas Barricade* was the winner and was so staged, under the direction of George McCowan with Zoe Caldwell in its cast, I recall. *The Canvas Barricade* did not live up to the great challenge and its failure seems to have discouraged the Festival from such new works—at least on this stage. But a lot has happened since 1961. The Canadian playwright has been paid a little more attention to. His output will have doubled this very year, under Centennial Commission urging. Now we have more playwrights, perhaps we will have more luck in finding a script that suits the new stage.

Perhaps *The Last of the Tsars,* which had to be written twice, was an unfortunate experience for the Festival in this matter of commissioning new works. But surely the success of *Colours in the Dark* has wiped out much of that. And *Colours in the Dark,* I think you might agree, could have

94

been staged in this Festival Theatre—even though its content seems, on first glance, to be so light and charming.

With two new artistic directors whose Canadian bias is a matter of fact not tact, the character and policies of the Festival will inevitably change—if not overnight. It is a matter of great importance—this change for Stratford's position as Canada's leading theatre makes it a flagship which will lead us all in new directions.

That is the extent of my speculation about Second Century Shakespeare—which turns out not to be the old Shakespeare at all but a new one yet to be found. I'm sorry I took so long to get to that conclusion but it did give me the opportunity to remind you of the growth of this Festival. And to point out that this theatre is—like the rest of Canada—at a turning point in its history in this Centennial year.

August 1967

VIOLA AND OTHER TRANSVESTIST HEROINES IN SHAKESPEARE'S COMEDIES

F. H. Mares

Shakespeare was an economical dramatist. He used certain stock characters, plot devices and theatrical situations over and over again. For example, it is part of the plot that a beloved woman is presumed dead when in fact she is still alive in *A Comedy of Errors, Romeo and Juliet, Much Ado, All's Well* and *Cymbeline*. In *Pericles* and *The Winter's Tale* this character is doubled, and both mother and daughter are lost and found. Sebastian thinks his dear sister dead in *Twelfth Night*. Cleopatra sends word to Antony that she is dead, and Othello has reason to fear the death of Desdemona in the storm that delays his own arrival in Cyprus. In half of these plays the loss or feared loss is associated with a storm at sea. Obviously these happenings are like each other only in the very simplest terms, but they still indicate that certain patterns of events preoccupied Shakespeare's imagination from the earliest to the latest of his plays, and this (if we can interpret it aright) may be very significant.

With theatrical situations which are similar, the resemblances are less simple—if only because the surrounding circumstances are more complicated. The presence of the audience must be understood, and their response to, and comprehension of, what they see and hear. Comparisons of this kind can be made in more detail and can be used to illustrate developments in Shakespeare's technique or changes in treatment appropriate to different kinds of drama. The recurrence of a stage situation, or set of situations, can still be read for the light it sheds on Shakespeare's psychology, but that is not my purpose here.

Shakespeare makes frequent use in his plays of a female disguised as a man. This is usually given in his source as part of the mechanism of the plot, and the 'Polly Oliver' who 'lists for a soldier to follow her love' is a common folk-lore figure, but in Shakespeare's handling these characters gain a theatrical force and importance that takes their disguise well beyond its simple plot function. I want to discuss four of these girls dressed as boys (and, of course, played by boys): Julia in *Two Gentlemen of Verona,* Rosalind in *As You Like It,* Viola in *Twelfth Night* and Imogen in *Cymbeline.* These are not the only examples, but Jessica's brief appearance as a page in *The Merchant of Venice* is a minor event in the play, and the disguise of Portia and Nerissa as lawyers is a special case, not the simple female-into-male transformation. Joan of Arc can hardly be said to be disguised at all. I would guess (and the assertion is no more scholarly than that) that the girl-boy figure is commoner in Shakespeare than in most of his contemporaries. There is a significant non-example in Jonson's Epicene, and it would be interesting to compare Shakespeare's handling with the much more sensational treatment of Euphrasia-Bellario in Beaumont and Fletcher's *Philaster.*

The girl-boy disguise is a special class of the general convention of disguise on the stage. For disguise to be theatrically effective, the *convention* must be accepted. The convention is that while we, the audience, recognize the disguised character with no difficulty at all, the other characters in the play never do so; and it is a convention of comedy rather than tragedy. Not exclusively, of course: Kent and Edgar take disguise in *King Lear,* but more commonly in tragedy disguise takes the form of dissimulation. The outward appearance is not changed, but the true character is concealed, as with the specious declarations of love for their father of Goneril and Regan, 'honest' Iago plotting against Othello, Hamlet's 'antic disposition', and so on. Comedy is more social, more artificial and more innocent, and so makes conventions like that of stage disguise more acceptable. Disguise is the premise from which all kinds of preposterous conclusions can be made to flow for our enjoyment and, when the game is over, all can be put straight by a simple act of disclosure which will leave no ill feelings.

Viola's is the most elaborate disguise of the four I wish to discuss. The convention asks us to accept not just that a girl in man's clothes should be taken for a young man, but that she should be actually indistinguishable from a particular young man, her brother, and that a lady of distinction should fall in love with him/her. This is broken to us slowly: first we have only Viola's intention to disguise herself as a man (and, incidentally, a eunuch, a suggestion never repeated), and the possibility that Sebastian is alive. It is only later that the living Sebastian appears, on his way to Orsino's court. Even so, it is a lot to swallow, and that we do swallow it means that we are particularly conscious in this play of the convention, of the tacit agreement between audience and players, to 'make believe'. 'This *is* Illyria, Lady.'

Harold Jenkins, in an elegant article (*Rice Institute Pamphlets*, XLV, 1959), has shown how closely the actions of *Twelfth Night* follow those of *Two Gentleman*. In each a girl disguised as a page in the service of the man she loves is sent by him as a messenger of love to another woman, and in both cases the love is rejected. Julia woos Sylvia for Proteus as Viola woos Olivia for Orsino. But the treatment of these similar situations (as Jenkins points out) is much more subtle and searching in the later play. In *Two Gentlemen* both girls behave in much the same way: they defy parents and convention to follow the men they love. Julia takes the disguise of a page, and

Sylvia calls on the protection (not in the event very useful) of Sir Eglamour. Julia simply follows her love, while Sylvia has the added motive of avoiding an unwanted lover. But Viola does not take on a boy's appearance to follow her lover: she does it as a form of protection in her own misfortune, and does not fall in love with Orsino until she is in his service. Olivia's behaviour is in marked contrast. She has refused love, and retired from the world, but when she sees Cesario she promptly makes her love clear to 'him'. When Sebastian appears, she does the proposing. There are few other women in Shakespeare who set the pace in lovemaking, and most of them are unpleasant. Tamora in *Titus,* Regan and Goneril in *Lear,* come to violent and deserved ends. Venus in *Venus and Adonis* is an immortal, but hardly a sympathetic character. Only Helena in *All's Well,* who combines modesty, virtue and medical skill with her curious desire to marry Bertram, is admirable and has a happy fate, but this is achieved only after much delay, a painful estrangement and the devious business of the proxy-bedding. Even then she must suffer a reported death and be resurrected in the disguise of another before being finally united with her husband. The Lady of the Strachey may have married the Yeoman of the Wardrobe with impunity, but Webster's Duchess of Malfi could not marry her Steward without disaster. On the whole, Olivia gets off very lightly: Malvolio thinks that she is making advances to him, and his presumption is ludicrous and unpardonable, but it is still, perhaps, something of a reflection on her.

The best known of Shakespeare's transvestist heroines—except, perhaps, for Viola herself—is Rosalind in *As You Like It*. Viola and Rosalind are alike in little more than their virtue and their disguises. Both become men to protect themselves, but Rosalind positively enjoys her disguise, flaunts it, exploits its possibilities, while Viola is embarrassed by it: 'Disguise, I see thou art a wickedness.' Rosalind proposes to have

> a swashing and a martial outside,
> As many other mannish cowards have
> That do outface it with their semblances,

but when a quarrel is forced on Viola, 'a little thing would make me tell them how much I lack of a man.' Rosalind uses her disguise to satisfy herself of Orlando's love, to enjoy it and at the same time to tease him; she uses it to teach Phebe a lesson in humility, and she engineers the conclusion, when the disguise is given up and the right pairs are united with each other. Rosalind plays proxy for herself, and is made love to by her own lover Orlando, though he does not know it. Viola goes as proxy for the man she loves to make love to another woman. In both cases the disguised woman has a superior consciousness of the situation, which the audience shares. For Rosalind the irony is joyful and a shade malicious; for Viola it is painful, and she herself is the sufferer. Because of the mistakes caused by her disguise, mistakes over which she has no control, Viola is humiliated in the quarrel with Sir Andrew and accused of ingratitude and cowardice by Antonio. In the final scene she appears to both Orsino and Olivia as false to them and a cowardly liar in her denials. When the revelation comes, it comes by chance and time: 'O time, thou must untangle this, not I.' Although, since the meeting with Antonio, Viola must have been almost certain that her brother was alive and in Illyria, she breathes not a word of this possibility, but waits for events to take their course.

Imogen's situation is more complicated. She is married, against her father's will, to Posthumus who is exiled. She runs away, as she thinks to join him, but in fact it is his plot to have her murdered because he thinks she has been unfaithful—which she has not. The plot is monstrously complicated, and seems to combine motifs from most of Shakespeare's plays: the calumny of *Much Ado* and *Othello,* the reported death of the woman and repentance of the offending male of *Much Ado, All's Well* and *The Winter's Tale,* the page disguise and the lost brother of *Twelfth Night,* the drug that produces the appearance of death and the awakening by the dead lover of *Romeo and Juliet,* and so on. In the final scene, when all the confusions are resolved, Imogen plays a part that combines something of both Rosalind and Viola. She appears as the page Fidele, and in this disguise sets in motion the unravelling. But in the disguise she also suffers at the hands of those she loves. Lucius, the Roman General, thinks her ungrateful, and the distraught Posthumus actually knocks her down. Only then, when it is thought for a moment that she is dead (for the third time in the play) is her true identity revealed. And then 'Pardon's the word for all,' she is reunited with her father Cymbeline, her long-lost brothers and her husband; only the wicked stepmother-queen and her beastly son are dead; the Britons, although they won the battle, agree to pay the 'wonted tribute' to the Romans, and they all live happily ever after!

It is amazing how much is packed into *Cymbeline*. One of the ways to think about these successive treatments of similar situations in Shakespeare is as a study in economy: each time the lemon is squeezed, more juice is got out of it. Dr. Johnson defended Shakespeare against the neo-classic critics of his time who thought that he should not have mixed comedy and tragedy by saying that this was like life: life is mixed good and bad, and so should art be. As consistently as he brought clowns into his tragedies Shakespeare brought pathos into his comedies. The fate of Egeon, condemned to death in the first scene, hangs over the farce of the *Comedy of Errors,* the news of the death of the Princess's father brings a shadow at the end of the gaiety of *Love's Labour's Lost,* and so on. *Two Gentlemen of Verona* is romance, the lovers are not comic. Julia's situation as she watches Proteus pay court to Sylvia is pathetic, and the love, even of the shifty Proteus, is taken entirely at face value:

PROTEUS: I likewise hear that Valentine is dead.

SILVIA: And so suppose am I; for in his grave
Assure thyself my love is buried.

PROTEUS: Sweet lady, let me rake it from the earth.

SILVIA: Go to thy lady's grave, and call hers thence,
Or at the least, in hers sepulchure thine.

JULIA: (*Aside*) He heard not that.

The comic aspects of love appear only in the clowns, as for example where the painful service of the lover to his lady is parodied by Launce's account of his sufferings for his dog. This parody by the clowns is present in *As You Like It* in Touchstone's affair with Audrey ('a poor thing, but mine own'), but this is only one of many patterns of love in that play and serves as a contrast to the romantic pastoral of Silvius and Phebe. Rosalind and Orlando do not need parody, for Rosalind provides it herself in her disguise as Ganymede. Although she is deeply in love she is aware of the limitations and absurdity of the state, and her gaiety gives them full expression.

ROSALIND: Well, in her person, I say, I will not have you.

ORLANDO: Then, in mine own person, I die.

ROSALIND: No, faith, die by attorney. The poor world is almost six thousand years old, and in all this time was not any man died in his own person, *videlicet,* in a love cause. . . . But these are all lies;

men have died from time to time, and worms
have eaten them, but not for love.

ORLANDO: I would not have my right Rosalind of this
mind, for I protest, her frown might kill me.

ROSALIND: By this hand, it will not kill a fly.

There is not in Viola's character scope for this kind of gaiety,
nor does her situation allow it. The absurdity of love, its
exaggeration, its disproportion to its object, which Rosalind's
light-hearted irony points out, is too painfully close to her:
the irony is in her situation:

I am the man—if it be so, as 'tis,
Poor lady, she were better love a dream. . . .
                    My master loves her dearly,
And I (poor monster!) fond as much on him:
And she, mistaken, seems to dote on me:
What will become of this? As I am man,
My state is desperate for my master's love;
As I am woman—now alas the day!—
What thriftless sighs shall poor Olivia breathe?

The situation is absurd, and both Orsino and Olivia are (in
their well-bred way) poseurs. The movement of the play
is to explode the poses and bring these two noble creatures
to a proper state of love. Viola (and her confusion with
Sebastian) is both the contrast to them and the instrument
of their reform. To make this effective a balance must be
kept between the pathos and the absurdity of her situation.
Consider how delicately this is done in Act II, Scene iv.
When Viola hints at her love for him, Orsino is condescend-
ing, and misses the point by miles.

ORSINO: What kind of woman is't?

VIOLA: Of your complexion.

ORSINO: She is not worth thee then. What years, i'faith?

VIOLA: About your years, my lord.

ORSINO: Too old, by heaven: let still the woman take
          An elder than herself; so wears she to him,
          So sways she level in her husband's heart:
          For, boy, however we do praise ourselves,
          Our fancies are more giddy and unfirm,
          More longing, wavering, sooner lost and won,
          Then women's are.

And after Feste's song he proves his point by contradicting himself:

> They lack retention,
> Alas, their love may be called appetite—
> No motion of the liver, but the palate—
> That suffers surfeit, cloyment and revolt;
> But mine is all as hungry as the sea,
> And can digest as much. Make no compare
> Between that love a woman can bear me
> And that I owe Olivia.

This is excellent fooling, and Feste is justified in his accusation that Orsino's 'mind is very opal', but it is combined with Viola's quiet assertions, and leads to her pathetic declaration, 'My father had a daughter loved a man.'

What I am trying to demonstrate is the increasing tightness of construction in these three situations, the increasing complexity of the emotional response we are obliged to make. Julia is romantic and pathetic and Launce is crudely funny, and the two responses are quite independent of each other, even though we may intellectually discover that they reflect on each other. Rosalind is romantic and wittily comic at the expense of her own and her lover's romanticism. She avoids pathos by undercutting its grounds, and it appears in the play only in the situation of old Adam and his devotion to Orlando. (In *Much Ado,* similarly, Beatrice and Benedict use their intelligent wit to avoid pathos, but this is strongly present in the situation of Hero.) In *Twelfth Night* pathos occurs in an essentially comic situation and arouses a curiously mixed response that is painful and yet allows a smile, but certainly removes the possibility of loud laughter. The laughter is displaced to the grosser aberrations of love in Sir Andrew and Malvolio.

In *Cymbeline* there is little comedy; feelings are raw and expressed with vehemence. Imogen's disguise as a boy is only a small part of a play with several varied and complex plots and themes that range from the personal through the political to the religious. Her sufferings are greater than those of any of the other girls in boy's clothing. She wakes from a drugged sleep (like Juliet) to find herself lying beside a headless body dressed in her husband's clothes. There is irony still in this scene, though it is a long way from comedy, but it is not felt either humourously or painfully by Imogen: it operates against her.

> A headless man!—The garments of Posthumus!
> I know the shape of's leg: this is his hand;
> His foot Mercurial; his Martial thigh;
> The brawns of Hercules: but his Jovial face—
> Murder in heaven?—How!—'Tis gone.—Pisanio,
> All curses madded Hecuba gave the Greeks,
> And mine to boot, be darted on thee! Thou,
> Conspired with that irregulous devil, Cloten,
> Hast here cut off my lord.

The body in fact is Cloten's, and Pisanio is the faithful servant still. The audience knows this but Imogen does not, nor does she know the terrible danger she has escaped. The relief we might feel at her escape, and the laughter at her mistaking the oaf Cloten for that paragon her husband, are inhibited by the horror of her situation and the intensity of her suffering, marvellously expressed in the emphatic broken rhythms of the verse, the impacted syntax and the piled hyperboles. More, and more violently opposed, feelings are evoked in this soliloquy of Imogen's than in the longer, more elegiac colloquy of Orsino and Viola.

These four episodes from Shakespeare's plays, where his boy players played girls pretending to be boys, show how, with increasing technical mastery, he became able to present more complex situations and elicit at the same time an increasing range of emotions in response from his audience. He can, indeed, provoke in us feelings that at first sight are opposed and seem mutually incompatible.

In all the examples except the last, the fact that the heroine is disguised as a boy is a significant part of the feeling of the scene. In the case of Imogen the disguise that operates is the dressing of Cloten's body in Posthumus's clothes. The disguise of Imogen operates ironically and to theatrical effect in the scenes with her unknown brothers, and also in the last scene, when Iachimo, her father who had blackened her reputation and Posthumus, her husband, all fail to recognize her. This reaches a climax when Posthumus strikes the interfering 'boy'. But so much has to be expounded in this scene that it is huddled up, and is much less effective than the steady build-up of feeling against Viola at the beginning of the fifth act of *Twelfth Night,* which is suddenly released with the appearance of Sebastian.[1] The disguise of Imogen is less theatrically important than the disguise in the other three plays. It is a device of the plot and not so specifically of the theatre. In the other plays the actual presence on stage of the girl who is pretending to be a boy (and was played by a boy) is part of the dramatic situation. Viola's double meanings are sharpened for us because we understand them, while the characters on stage do not. This technique brings

1 I have never seen a more moving presentation of the recognition of Viola and Sebastian than that at Stratford (Ontario) in 1966. It showed, better than any argument, how close this scene is to the great reconciliation at the end of *The Winter's Tale.*

its highest delights in *As You Like It,* when Rosalind in disguise as Ganymede plays herself in mockery with Orlando, but it is present even in the tedious musical puns of Act I, Scene ii of *Two Gentlemen.*

It is not very valuable to say that one play of Shakespeare's is better or worse than another. I have suggested an increasing complexity of feeling in the scenes in chronological sequence. Now I wish to use this comparison of four plays, in which the situation of a girl disguised as a boy, in love with a man who does not recognize her or her true sex occurs, to elucidate to some extent the particular quality of each play. *Twelfth Night* was written about the turn of the sixteenth century, when Shakespeare was at the height of his powers, yet it is usually considered the last of his comedies. Later plays which follow the traditional action of comedy—the vicissitudes of love ending in marriage—are 'dark' comedies (*Measure for Measure*) or romances. Their emotional texture is quite different. *Twelfth Night* concerns a melancholy Duke, a mourning Lady, a shipwrecked and bereaved girl; the pathos of the situation of the central character is considerable, and the play ends with a song that insists on a dismal view of human nature and the weather, and yet we know that happiness is possible in Illyria in a way that is not possible in Vincentio's Vienna, and can be achieved at much less cost than in *The Winter's Tale.* The way in which the convention of disguise is handled is important in giving us this assurance. It involves the audience in a kind of complicity with what is going forward on the stage; we have a fuller knowledge than any of the characters. It is worth noting how cunningly the first appearance of Sebastian is timed. He appears in the interval while Malvolio is following Viola with the ring from Olivia: directly after Olivia has declared her love for 'Cesario', and directly before Viola admits her love for Orsino. Before the complications really begin we are assured that the solution is at hand. So far as the main plot is concerned, all the actions of *Twelfth Night* arise from Viola's disguise, from her taking the appearance of the brother she believes dead. All her humiliation and pain arise from an action of her own which is prudent in the circumstances— nobody else wittingly inflicts pain on her. Because we know that a solution is available, while we share her pathos and admire the courage and integrity with which she meets her misfortunes, we can also laugh at the mistakes and confusions that arise. When Sebastian finally appears all the confusions and misunderstandings disappear. The main plot of *Twelfth Night* is beautiful. It is like a soap-bubble: it rises from the single assumption that Sebastian is dead, and when that is proved false the bubble bursts and there is nothing left of the animosities and confusions that arose from the false assumption.

By contrast, the scenes in *As You Like It* of Rosalind as Ganymede with Orlando, though delightful in themselves, are gratuitous in terms of plot. The only reason for Rosalind to conceal her identity from Orlando is that she chooses to do so. In this as in so much else, once she has left Duke Frederick's court, she controls the action. Danger and certain kinds of suffering are left outside the forest, and the real evil that appears in Oliver and Frederick is quite arbitrarily reformed. The source of *As You Like It* is a romance, but it is treated anti-romantically. Where *Twelfth Night* has a plot structure of high comedy arising from disguise, the essential structure of *As You Like It* is intellectual. The meaning of the play is in the juxtaposition of a whole series of attitudes to love. This meaning is most explicitly stated in the repartee of 'Ganymede' and Orlando. Rosalind's disguise frees her to say for herself and for us what she could not with propriety say in her own person.

The heroine's disguise has a less important place in *Two*

Gentlemen and *Cymbeline*. Julia's disguise does little more than offer opportunities for pathos; the comedy of situation hardly develops, since her double-meanings are played with the Host (who goes to sleep), and the complications of the plot are caused by Proteus' dissimulation and not by her disguise. Her true identity is revealed at the end of the play, but does nothing to make more acceptable the notoriously abrupt reform of Proteus. No such facile resolution is found in *Cymbeline*. Though there is reconciliation all round and repentance for Iachimo, the passions have been too strong and the suffering too great to be controlled within comedy. The complications of the plot have come not only from disguise and mistaken identity but also from dissimulation and malice. Antonio's harsh words to 'Cesario', accusing him of ingratitude and cowardice, disappear as soon as Sebastian appears: there is nothing to forgive. But Posthumus's attempt to have Imogen murdered, though it may be explained by Iachimo's confession, still remains and has to be forgiven. In *Two Gentlemen* and *Cymbeline* the disguise of the girl as a boy provides good scenes but is not integral to the plot (as in *Twelfth Night*), nor essential to the statement of the theme (as in *As You Like It*): they are less economical examples of a theatrical situation that Shakespeare made much use of.

August 1966

TWELFTH NIGHT

Charles Tyler Prouty

In some thirty years of teaching it has been my experience that of all the plays in the Shakespeare canon the comedies are the most difficult to teach. The Joyous Comedies in particular require so much explanation that we are in danger of losing the play in establishing what I regard as the essential details. The reason is very simply that these are sophisticated plays based on a complex of social and literary conventions that were well known to the Renaissance world in general and the Elizabethan world in particular but are almost unknown to our world. In *Twelfth Night* we are dealing almost exclusively with the conventions of love and the behaviour of lovers—conventions which are completely alien to our world. The important thing, however, is Shakespeare's reaction to these conventions, which controls the nature of his play and makes it, therefore, peculiarly his own. In the social world of the Renaissance the traditions of the Middle Ages which we call Courtly Love flourished, and these conventions were incredibly sophisticated; they are not certainly, to be seen in the context of the banal sexuality of our times.

For example, in the 1570s a *novella* by George Whetstone entitled 'Rinaldo and Giletta' tells us a lovely story. An aged man by the name of Frizaldo is in love with the fair Giletta, but Giletta is not in love with him. Rather she is in love with Rinaldo, a handsome but poor young man who is, of course, in love with her. On a specific occasion Frizaldo has entered

Giletta's chamber while Rinaldo is outside underneath the balcony singing a love song. Frizaldo, recognizing the voice, pretends ignorance as far as Giletta is concerned, and so he addresses her with the term of 'Mistress'. Giletta, in order to conceal her knowledge of the singer outside, is forced to use the appropriate reply: she addresses Frizaldo as 'Servant'. These words, 'Servant' and 'Mistress', are conventional words and do not necessarily imply a sexual relationship; but the implication is enough for the wretched Rinaldo, who flees the scene and jumps into the river, ostensibly to die. But, perhaps because of the temperature of the water or for some other reason, he has second thoughts, swims to the farthest shore, returns in the nick of time to rescue the fair Giletta, and all ends happily! The conventions in this kind of story are typical, and, for example, we see in the second scene of *Twelfth Night,* where the ship captain tells Viola, 'What great ones do, the less will prattle of,' that the types of behaviour reflected here were not exclusively the property of the great; while the great had established the game, the game itself was known through all strata of society. However by the 1590s the game had become the subject of witty scoffing. For example, in Greene's *Menaphon,* first published in 1589, we find these lines from 'Doron's Eclogue ioynd with Carmela's'. Doron addresses Carmela:

> Carmela *deare, euen as the golden ball*
> *That* Venus *got, such are thy goodly eyes,*
> *When cherries iuice is iumbled therewithall,*
> *Thy breath is like the steeme of apple pies.*

> *Thy lippes resemble Two Cowcumbers faire,*
> *Thy teeth like to the tuskes of fattest swine,*
> *Thy speach is like the thunder in the aire:*
> *Would God thy toes, thy lips and all were mine.*

Here we can see how the conventional epithets of 'ruby lips' and 'pearl-like teeth' have been reduced to rustic figures, and thus how the whole game is deliberately undercut and becomes the subject of laughter. The same kind of thing occurs in *As You Like It* when Rosalind tells Orlando, 'Men have died from time to time and worms have eaten them but not for love.' This, of course, is a great blow to the over-serious Orlando because he really does believe that he would die from love, even though he fails to keep his appointments with Rosalind in spite of all his oaths. And Rosalind has played with the conventions still further with her references to Troilus's having his brains dashed out with a Grecian club and Leander's being drowned by catching a cramp on a hot summer's night. The whole set of conventions was understood by the Elizabethans (and as a matter of fact it was still understood in pre-war England as we can see in such a play as Noel Coward's *Private Lives* or in the popular press. Such periodicals as the *Tatler* were filled with pictures of the 'great ones' at balls, at hunts, at race meetings and all that sort of thing, and these were largely seized upon by the middle and lower classes as subjects for conversation and objects of admiration.)

The conventions are clearly indicated in the source materials of *Twelfth Night* so we must know about these materials and must try to ascertain Shakespeare's comprehension of them, what he read and also what he knew about the intellectual milieu in which these conventions operated and out of which the written materials came.

The first mention of *Twelfth Night*, in John Manningham's *Diary*, is in the entry for 2 February 1602. At the Middle Temple the Candlemas Feast was celebrated by a performance which Manningham describes as 'a play called Twelve Night or What You Will, much like the Commedy of Errores, or Menechmi in Plautus, but most like and neere to that in Italian called *Inganni*.'

The latter play to which Manningham refers is an Italian

play of 1562 written by one Nicolo Secchi. More important for our purposes, however, is the earliest known play dealing with the theme of separated twins; this, *Gl'Ingannati,* first printed in 1537, was presented by the Academy of the Intronnati of Siena—Intronnati, of course, means 'Thunderstruck'. In its printed form it was preceded by another play, a comedy entitled the *Comedia del Sacrificio,* which was also a presentation of the Thunderstruck Ones. Here the members all appear as rebels against the tyranny of love. In the centre of the stage is a large urn with a fire burning inside and each member of the Academy in turn makes his way forward to cast into the urn some token of his erstwhile beloved so that it is consumed by the flames and thus symbolizes his rejection of love. He, of course, speaks appropriate lines to indicate what he is doing and why he is doing it.

Now this Academy is not something unusual. It was one of many that spread all over Italy during the late fifteenth and early sixteenth century, and these derived from the fifteenth-century Platonic Academy in Florence which was a very serious Academy (for example, Ficino's Commentary on Plato's *Symposium* was only one of the works that came out of it). The serious purpose was, however, very soon lost and the jesting spirit took over. Practically every city in Italy had an Academy by the sixteenth century, and the custom of such academies spread to even France and Germany. The aim had now become one of producing courtiers in imitation of *Il Cortegiano,* polished and refined gentlemen. The names of the societies and of the individual members became wittily allegorical or symbolic. Wit was prized above all, everything was a subject for jesting.

It is just such an academy as this that we find in Shakespeare's *Love's Labour's Lost* or in the festivities at Gray's Inn, entitled *Gesta Grayorum.* Now let us turn to the play of the 'Thunderstruck Ones'. It's a typical Italian comedy of plot, the

Commedia Erudita. There is no attention paid to character or morality; the play is amoral. Most important there is no tone except the tone of jesting and a complete lack of seriousness. This is the most important aspect that we have to consider in *Twelfth Night*—the whole aspect of tone.

Specifically the immediate English source is a short story by Barnaby Riche, 'Apollonius and Scilla', contained in a collection which Riche wrote and entitled *Riche His Farewell to the Militarie profession,* printed in 1581. Riche's point of view is quite different from that of the Italians and, of course, from that of Shakespeare. He has gathered together these stories, according to his own word, for 'the onely delight of the courteous Gentlewomen bothe of England and Ireland'. Riche is, in short, a bourgeois moralist who, as a very moral gentleman, takes a very dim view of the whole game of Love. In his own preface to the volume he speaks of the poisoned cup of error, love being madness, wickedness, etc., etc. But we do not need to labour that point, it will appear later.

Exactly as Riche began his story with comments on love in general so did Shakespeare, but with what a difference: 'If music be the food of love, play on, Give me excess of it . . .' (It's interesting that Kemble transposed this scene, made it the second scene, and made Viola's appearance, which we find in scene two of modern editions, the first—Sir Tyrone Guthrie did the same thing in his production at this Stratford.) This is, of course, a gross misunderstanding of the play because one needs this first scene to set the tone of the whole play. The problem is, of course, how we are to read this soliloquy of Orsino's. It can be read as 'big' lyric poetry, with high soaring gestures, and so on, or perhaps, more wisely, it can be read with a certain degree of archness which will give the audience an idea of a slight undercutting. As a matter of fact, the whole show is given away by the Duke's final lines, 'So full of shapes is fancy / That it alone is high fantastical,' which are immediately followed by Curio's inquiry, 'Will you go hunt, my lord?'

DUKE: What, Curio?

CURIO: The hart.

DUKE: Why, so I do, the noblest that I have.
        O, when mine eyes did see Olivia first,
        Methought she purged the air of pestilence.
        That instant was I turned into a hart,
        And my desires, like fell and cruel hounds,
        E'er since pursue me.

The reference was obvious to anybody in Shakespeare's audience because even the middle classes would have read Ovid in school. They would have known that the learned Duke was referring to the myth of Actaeon who gazed upon Diana bathing and was punished by being pursued by his own hounds after a vengeful Diana metamorphosed him into a stag.

The same kind of learned reference is found in the ensuing dialogue when Valentine reports about Olivia's reaction to the Duke's suit. The key here is, of course, in the language and the way it is used. Valentine knows the proper words: 'And water once a day her chamber round with high offending brine.' But the Duke does even better:

    O, she that hath a heart of that fine frame
    To pay this debt of love but to a brother,
    How will she love when the rich golden shaft
    Hath killed the flock of all affections else
    That live in her; when liver, brain, and heart,
    These sovereign thrones, are all supplied and filled,
    Her sweet perfections, with one self king.
    Away before me to sweet beds of flow'rs;
    Love-thoughts lie rich when canopied with bow'rs.

In other words, Orsino has read all the right books. The

'rich golden shaft' is, of course, Cupid's arrow. He has two sets of arrows, gold and lead; the gold inspires love, the lead inspires dislike, or to use the Elizabethan word, disdain. Furthermore, it is not just a golden arrow, it is a rich, golden shaft. And Orsino continues to demonstrate his knowledge as well as his imaginative powers. The seats of her affections are thoroughly described, 'liver, brain, and heart'—the 'sovereign thrones'.

Now according to various theories of love, the seat of the affections could be any one of these three parts of the body—usually the heart, though of course the liver and brain figured too. But Orsino has to get them all in just to prove how learned he really is. Here then is a key to the whole play. The use of language, the words, the conceits, the figures, the references, but most important the way in which these are used and the tone in which they are spoken, is exemplified for us quite clearly, I think, by what I have said about Curio's entry, the Ovid reference, Cupid's arrows and the seats of the affections.

We find the same tone in Viola's first appearance in the second scene:

VIOLA: What country, friends, is this?
CAPTAIN: This is Illyria, lady.
VIOLA: And what should I do in Illyria?
           My brother he is in Elysium.

Having consigned her brother to the other world, Viola at once imagines that he is not dead. 'Perchance he is not drowned. What think you, sailors?' One notes the three 'perchances' in three successive lines: 'perchance he is not drowned'; the captain replies that it is 'perchance' she was saved; Viola replies, 'O my poor brother, and so perchance may he be.' This is no accident; this is another perfectly clear clue to an Elizabethan audience, as it should be to us, that games are going on. The game continues with the Captain, who refers to her brother whom he had seen clinging to a mast

> Where like Arion on the dolphin's back,
> I saw him hold acquaintance with the waves
> So long as I could see.

The Captain is learned, he knows his classical mythology too. The story of Arion and the dolphin was well known. This matter of tone is further evidenced by the way in which coincidence now takes over. It just so happens that the Captain was born near where they have been cast up on the seacoast and he knows all about Orsino. So, too, does Viola. 'Orsino! I have heard my father name him. He was a bachelor then.' (One notices Viola's first reference, 'He was a bachelor then.' Her 'fell and cruel' intent is quite clear!)

Following the Captain's reference to Olivia and his description of her, Viola momentarily forgets about the bachelor. Now she is going to serve this lady who has retired from the world and whose sad condition suits with Viola's. However, she immediately changes her mind again and decides to serve Orsino, of course in disguise. She is going to be a eunuch to account for her voice, and the Captain is to introduce her and to secure her a position in Orsino's service. As far as this matter of tone is concerned, the exit line is interesting. Viola says, 'I thank thee. Lead me on.' Well, what a way to end the scene!

Let us follow this whole matter of tone in the main plot. Viola next appears in Act I, Scene iv, where she is going under the assumed masculine name of Cesario. She is very high in the Duke's favour, so high in fact that she is to go a-wooing for him: 'I'll do my best to woo your lady.' But suddenly we are struck over the head by her concluding lines, with their nice use of couplet, in an aside, 'Yet a barful strife! Whoe'er I woo, myself would be his wife.'

In all the typical Elizabethan romances this is the way they fall in love. It is a *coup de foudre*—all of a sudden they are in love. This is the first we have heard of Viola's love. We might have anticipated it, but the way in which it is delivered to us gives us the tone of the play and the tone with which we are expected to approach the love portions of the play.

But it most certainly should be noted that, although we are dealing with a convention, the language of Viola here, and of other characters in similar situations, is not stylized, not a language of conventions. Here we have a plain style, with a simple, bare, statement of fact. Elsewhere when Viola is dealing with other conventions she can use an imaginative language, a poetic language, but here in her declaration of love, she does not.

The next time we meet Viola is toward the end of the first act. Here she has come a-wooing for Orsino, but the scene has begun with our introduction to the lady Olivia whose first line, to us, is 'Take the fool away' (referring, of course, to the Clown, Feste), In the ensuing dialogue with Feste and Malvolio there is no evidence whatsoever of Olivia's great sorrow of which we have heard so much but which she never displays. Feste does ask her why she mourns, but she makes merely a brief and undeveloped factual response to this. Olivia ticks off Malvolio, she greets the drunken Sir Toby rather easily and her big moment comes, as I have said, when Viola comes a-wooing for Orsino.

This encounter between Viola (Cesario) and Olivia is what I choose to call the 'Big Game' scene, because in this scene both Viola and Olivia know that each is playing a game and each one of them knows that the other knows that respective roles are being performed. Just to make sure that we do not miss the point Viola begins by referring to herself as an actor: 'I would be loath to cast away my speech; for, besides that it is excellently well penned, I have taken great pains to con it.' In other words, she has a set speech which she has ostensibly written herself and which she has learned by heart. The same figure of an actor is carried on in the ensuing dialogue when Olivia inquires, 'Are you a comedian?' 'No', says Viola, 'no, my profound heart; and yet (by the very fangs of malice I swear) I am not that I play.' A few lines later she again refers to her speech, 'Alas, I took great pains to study it, and 'tis poetical.' An actual definition of her role is found when she says, 'I am a messenger.' She subsequently uses, of course, the language of heraldry, as does Olivia. And here the dialogue gives a clear indication of the nature and intention of the scene, when Olivia says, 'Sure you have some hideous matter to deliver, when the courtesy of it is so fearful. Speak your office' (the office of herald). One notes the adjectives 'hideous' and 'fearful'; such matters, of course, are not for everyone's ears, and so Viola makes it quite clear that she will only speak to Olivia: 'It alone concerns your ear. I bring no overture of war, no taxation of homage. I hold the olive in my hand. My words are as full of peace as matter.' These are the phrases, the conventional phrases, of a herald.

Olivia opens the next gambit by inquiring, 'Now, sir, what is your text?', to which Viola replies, 'Most sweet lady—'. Olivia: 'A most comfortable doctrine, and much may be said of it. Where lies your text?' Now the use of this word 'text' is a definite reminder of the language of love, which is part of the amalgamation of the Petrarchan tradition with that of Courtly Love in which the lover becomes an almost religious figure and the lady, of course, a saint. (Near the beginning of his career in *The Two Gentlemen of Verona* Shakespeare uses this religious conceit in connection with love in the dialogue in the very first scene between Valentine and Proteus.) The conceits continue. In answer to the inquiry, 'Where lies your text?' Viola replies, 'In Orsino's bosom.' Olivia asks, 'In his bosom? In what chapter of his bosom?'

To which Viola replies, 'To answer by the method, in the first of his heart.' Thus the figure of the 'text' of her message has been related to Orsino's heart. Olivia is playing along and uses the word 'chapter', referring, of course, to 'text'; one is curious as to just what Viola means by the 'method'. Certainly she doesn't mean 'method' in the modern sense of 'mumble and scratch'; she means 'method' in following the conventions. This is the way you play the Game; this is what you ought to say.

Viola's next move is to ask to see Olivia's face, and Viola can be a little bit arch or, to some people's tastes, almost cruel. When she comments on the vision of Olivia's beauty, 'Excellently done, if God did all,' Olivia insists, ''Tis in grain sir; 'twill endure wind and weather.' Says Viola,

> 'Tis beauty truly blent, whose red and white
> Nature's own sweet and cunning hand laid on.
> Lady, you are the cruell'st she alive
> If you will lead these graces to the grave,
> And leave the world no copy.

(We are at once reminded of similar ideas in Shakespeare's *Sonnets* where the friend is urged to marry so that his beauty may be passed on through his children to subsequent generations and thus not be lost to the world.) Well, this is rather old stuff by about 1600, the probable date of *Twelfth Night*. Olivia is not going to have much more of this, and solves the problem of preserving her beauty by saying,

> O, sir, I will not be so hard-hearted. I will give out divers schedules of my beauty. It shall be inventoried, and every particle and utensil labelled to my will: as, item, two lips, indifferent red; item, two grey eyes, with lids to them; item, one neck, one chin, and so forth. Were you sent hither to praise me?

Beauty has thus been reduced to an inventory such as one might find appended to an *inquisition post mortem* or in a testamentary paper such as a will. The conceit that Olivia is here employing punctures, of course, any idealization of love. It completely destroys the traditional description of a beautiful woman derived from Ariosto's description of Alcina, one that begins at the forehead and proceeds down to the eyebrows, the eyes, the nose, the lips, the teeth, the throat and so on.

Olivia thinks rather well of Orsino:

> Yet I suppose him virtuous, know him noble,
> Of great estate, of fresh and stainless youth;
> In voices well divulged, free, learned, and valiant,
> And in dimension and the shape of nature
> A gracious person. But yet I cannot love him.
> He might have took his answer long ago.

At this point Viola remembers her speech and launches into it when Olivia inquires, 'Why, what would you?'

> Make me a willow cabin at your gate
> And call upon my soul within the house;
> Write loyal cantons of contemned love
> And sing them loud even in the dead of night;
> Halloe your name to the reverberate hills
> And make the babbling gossip of the air
> Cry out 'Olivia!' O, you should not rest
> Between the elements of air and earth
> But you should pity me.

This lyric strain is soon ended by Olivia whose only comment is, 'You might do much. What is your parentage?'

VIOLA: Above my fortunes, yet my state is well.
          I am a gentleman.

OLIVIA: Get you to your lord.
          I cannot love him. Let him send no more.

Viola does her best to preserve the traditional love strain:

> Love makes his heart of flint that you shall love;
> And let your fervor, like my master's, be
> Placed in contempt. Farewell, fair cruelty.

121

And with only a few more words than Viola has used to inform us of her love for Orsino, Olivia tells us that she has fallen in love with Viola in her guise of Cesario:

> Not too fast; soft, soft,
> Unless the master were the man. How now?
> Even so quickly may one catch the plague?
> Methinks I feel this youth's perfections
> With an invisible and subtle stealth
> To creep in at mine eyes.

And, at the conclusion, 'Well, let it be.' This is all we hear. She has fallen love; there is nothing much to be done about it. Well, let it be.

The ring episode concludes this part of our study. Olivia has sent Malvolio in pursuit of Viola-Cesario, telling him that the ring had been left with her by Cesario, presumably as a gift from Orsino. Of course, no such ring has appeared. This is simply a device of Olivia's, and Viola quite understands what's going on when she encounters Malvolio. Here again the language is very important. Viola says:

> She loves me sure; the cunning of her passion
> Invites me in this churlish messenger.
> None of my lord's ring? Why he sent her none.
> I am the man. If it be so, as 'tis,
> Poor lady, she were better love a dream.
> Disguise, I see thou art a wickedness
> Wherein the pregnant enemy does much.
> How easy is it for the proper false
> In women's waxen hearts to set their forms!
> Alas, our frailty is the cause, not we,
> For such as we are made of, such we be.

There can be no question that in the terms 'pregnant enemy' and 'proper false' we have a reference to Satan, but what is such a serious reference doing in such a context? Well, very simply in my view it emphasizes the whole artificiality of

the episode that we have witnessed—the game that Olivia
and Viola have been playing with one another. And this
artificiality is, of course, emphasized by the couplet with
which Viola ends the scene:

> O Time, thou must untangle this, not I;
> It is too hard a knot for me t' untie.

Again the couplet rhyme, again the bald statement of fact—
nothing much can be done about it, time just has to work
it out somehow or other. This final couplet, like Viola's
couplet announcing her love for Orsino, is in the best
tradition of the romances, exactly the sort of thing that we
find in *Two Gentlemen of Verona* over and over again. The
point is that we are laughing at, or are amused by, the whole
business. The ultimate absurdity in this play is found in the
denouement. The Duke learning of Olivia's love, is ready
to kill Cesario. He breaks forth:

> O thou dissembling cub, what wilt thou be
> When time hath sowed a grizzle on thy case?
> Or will not else thy craft so quickly grow
> That thine own trip shall be thine overthrow?
> Farewell, and take her; but direct thy feet
> Where thou and I, henceforth, may never meet.

About a hundred lines later, after Sebastian has appeared and
the mystery of the identity has cleared up, the Duke is very
anxious to marry Viola:

> Give me thy hand,
> And let me see thee in thy woman's weeds.

Here again a declaration of love is couched in very, very
simple language, lacking ornamentation or imagery of any
sort: 'Let me see thee in thy woman's weeds.' This is no
'big' confession of love, no 'big lyric love stuff' whatsoever.
In fact, the nearest we come to any traditional language is
found when the Duke says,

Here is my hand; you shall from this time be
Your master's mistress.

We may now, I think, briefly summarize the main plot.
We have been operating in a world of artificiality. The
whole question of reality has been raised by Viola. The
business of falling in love is completely artificial. The switch
of the Duke is completely artificial. The characters themselves are not, in the accepted sense of the word, rounded,
three-dimensional characters. They are, in essence, flat, but
this does not mean that Shakespeare has lacked dramatic
skill—far from it. He is using these characters for his own
purposes. He is playing games with us, and, by playing
games, he convinces us of the reality of the characters. Of
course we like Viola. She is a very sweet girl, but there is no
depth to the character, no dimension to it beyond the purely
theatrical. In other words, we are dealing here with theatrical
truth as opposed to the truth of the printed page. The illusion
in the theatre will hold us, will captivate us, and, in the
theatre, no more is needed for this artificial love. It's exactly
the sort of thing that Noel Coward does to perfection. In
other words, I am suggesting that we treat the play as a play
and examine it on the basis of its theatrical premises. Here
these premises are the artificial world of lovers as exemplified
over and over again in the world of Queen Elizabeth's
court where such games were played, such lines spoken,
such attitudes taken; and everything turns out all right, of
course.

As we turn to the subplot we find ourselves in a very real
world indeed. Sir Toby and Sir Andrew are drunk every
night. Toby is, of course, urging Sir Andrew on, ostensibly
to woo Olivia, but mainly because Sir Andrew has three
thousand ducats a year. The hypocrisy of Toby's attitude
toward Sir Andrew and his possible wooing of Olivia is
found in his description of Sir Andrew: 'He's as tall a man

as any's in Illyria'—'tall' suggesting a 'fine, upstanding noble fellow'. Furthermore, according to Toby, Sir Andrew has other gifts: 'He plays o' th' viol-de-gamboys, and speaks three or four languages word for word without book, and hath all the good gifts of nature.' But immediately Sir Andrew appears his stupidity is apparent in his misunderstanding of Toby's simple injunction, 'Accost', which he takes to be Maria's name. As far as being a musician or having other talents, as far as languages go, Sir Andrew denies them specifically in his own words. For example, he says, 'Methinks sometimes I have no more wit than a Christian or an ordinary man has. But I am a great eater of beef, and I believe that does harm to my wit.' A few lines later he demonstrates his complete ignorance of foreign languages when Toby inquires, 'Pourquoi, my dear knight?' 'What is pourquoi?' asks Andrew, 'Do, or not do? I would I had bestowed that time in the tongues that I have in fencing, dancing, and bear-baiting. O, had I but followed the arts!' Sir Toby's original description of Andrew in terms of the courtier, the gentleman, is completely invalidated by Andrew himself. He is rather the exact opposite of the ideal courtier, the ideal courtly gentleman. When describing his abilities in dancing, in response to Toby's inquiry, 'What is thy excellence in a galliard, knight?' 'Faith, I can cut a caper,' says Sir Andrew; and he goes on, 'And I think I have the back-trick simply as strong as any man in Illyria.' Toby hits back very, very hard: 'Wherefore are these things hid?' These things are, of course, not assets; they are not recommendations for Sir Andrew as a potential suitor for the fair Olivia—far from it.

If Sir Andrew is a caricature, so too is Malvolio. But Malvolio has the further distinction of being rather unpleasant. We see this unpleasantness quite clearly in the later scene when Sir Toby and the others are having a good time drinking and singing and eating:

> My masters, are you mad? Or what are you? Have you
> no wit, manners, nor honesty, but to gabble like tinkers
> at this time of night? Do ye make an alehouse of my
> lady's house, that ye squeak out your coziers' catches
> without any mitigation or remorse of voice? Is there
> no respect of place, persons, nor time in you?

Here Malvolio's attitude is well described in Toby's line,
'Dost thou think, because thou art virtuous, there shall be
no more cakes and ale?'

Malvolio is the enemy of joy, of cakes and ale, of pleasure
in life. This has tempted some to press, I think, just a bit too
hard on Malvolio as a portrait of a Puritan. No, no! Olivia
is much more accurate when, earlier in the play, she has told
Malvolio, 'You are sick of self-love.'

And it is this very state of mind, this being sick of self-love,
that motivates the action of the subplot. Here we note that
in contrast with the main plot we do have specific motivation.
Things happen now for a reason. The letter is planted in
order to gull and trick Malvolio. The characters involved
are in a sense lowlife and quite realistic. Thus we have the
artificial world of Orsino and Olivia and Viola, in contrast
with the world in the servants' hall. In both plots we see
foolish love, but in the artificial world everything works
out all right. We need a bit of machinery to get Antonio out
of trouble. And, obviously, there has got to be some
machinery to get Malvolio out of gaol. But it cannot be too
strongly emphasized that there is no machinery of this
nature in the main plot; there we have simply the *deus ex
machina* appearance of Sebastian to resolve the question of
identity and all is well.

We must not leave the play without some mention of the
note of sadness which has received so much comment.
Reviewing a recent performance at Stratford-upon-Avon,
Harold Hobson of the *Sunday Times* described *Twelfth Night*

as Shakespeare's most melancholy play and also as his most wittily written.

The melancholy is found exclusively in Feste's songs, in the first:

> O mistress mine, where are you roaming?
> O, stay and hear! your true-love's coming,
>   That can sing both high and low.
> Trip no further, pretty sweeting;
>   Journeys end in lovers meeting,
>   Every wise man's son doth know;

and the conclusion of the second verse,

> Then come kiss me, sweet and twenty,
>   Youth's a stuff will not endure.

To suit the Duke's melancholy of love Feste produces another famous song:

> Come away, come away, death,
> And in sad cypress let me be laid.

And, of course, perhaps the most famous song is that which concludes the play when Feste sings:

> When that I was and a little tiny boy,
>   With hey, ho, the wind and the rain,
> A foolish thing was but a toy,
>   For the rain it raineth every day.

I think we should, perhaps, temper our attitude towards this note of sadness with reference to the title of the play, *Twelfth Night or What You Will*. Twelfth Night, the Feast of the Epiphany, marked the end of the Christmas festivities and, as a general rule, there was no more playing of plays at Court until the Sunday before the beginning of Lent or on Shrove Tuesday itself. Thus very simply Twelfth Night marks the end of the festivities of the Christmas season. In that sense it is not too difficult to understand that final stanza of the last song.

> A great while ago the world begun,
>   With hey, ho, the wind and the rain;
> But that's all one, our play is done,
>   And we'll strive to please you every day.

The fun and the games are over and we will have one last fling, a sort of carnival time before Lent—but that is still some weeks away. In other words, I don't think we need to be any more seriously concerned about it than I have indicated. The title—The End of the Christmas Revelry. Yes, yes. It's all over—the fun and games are ended. And so Adieu.

August 1966

JULIUS CAESAR

Arnold Edinborough

Shakespeare is, of all great geniuses, the one who is deepest embedded in his own cultural soil. The scene may be indicated as Padua or Verona, but the actions and talk seem suspiciously like Clerkenwell or Moorfields. When Theseus calls for the Athenian youth to entertain him, they are found to be led by a roaring boy from, perhaps, Hounslow, who is called Bottom even by his friends, and plain Ass by more ethereal beings.

But it is not just the manner of Shakespeare's plays, it is also the matter which is English. In that spectacular first decade of Shakespeare's writing career which stretches from 1589 to 1599, exactly half of the eighteen plays he wrote deal directly with English history. What is more, they deal with English history in an othodox fashion: first come the three parts of *Henry VI* to show that to be a good king a man has to be able to use the power which he inherits; then comes *Richard III* to show that to be a bad king he has to abuse the power which he inherits, and that finally, no matter which side a man fails on, a good Tudor nobleman like your own Queen's grandfather can quickly put the throne back to rights.

Having thus proclaimed himself a loyal subject as well as a good playwright, Shakespeare takes off to Syracuse for the *Comedy of Errors,* Verona for the *Two Gentlemen* and *Romeo,* and to France to show how *Love's Labours* can be *Lost*.

This overseas excursion, however, palls, and like many a

gentleman of his day (and later), he feels all the more in love with England when he does come back. Within six months of leaving the Capulet monument, his Muse is proclaiming its provenance in ringing tones:

> This royal throne of kings, this scepter'd isle,
> This earth of majesty, this seat of Mars,
> This other Eden, demi-paradise,
> This fortress built by Nature for herself
> Against infection and the hand of war,
> This happy breed of men, this little world,
> This precious stone set in the silver sea,
> Which serves it in the office of a wall
> Or as a moat defensive to a house,
> Against the envy of less happier lands,
> This blessed plot, this earth, this realm, this England.

And, a year later, a new kind of Englishman—rough in speech and tough in character—a proper bastard—is ending another play with sentiments more succinct but no less powerful:

> This England never did, nor never shall,
> Lie at the proud foot of a conqueror,
> But when it first did help to wound itself,
> Now these her princes are come home again,
> Come the three corners of the world in arms,
> And we shall shock them. Nought shall make us rue,
> If England to itself do rest but true.

There follows another excursion abroad. Then, in no time, Shakespeare is back on the battlefield. The kings are farther back in time, but the problems being discussed are even more relevant to the age: the divine right of kings; the necessity to exercise that right; the required ability to know the people as well as rule them; the solemn duty to breed to ensure the dynasty by primogeniture and due of birth.

As well as the schemes of Kings and Counsellors, we have,

in both parts of *Henry IV,* the antics of the *hoi polloi,* and of the son of a man who took the throne by force; in *Henry V,* we have the Renaissance ideal of a prince. In the first place he is morally invulnerable because he inherits his throne. God, through his father's big battalions, is now even more firmly on his family's side. (In the Tudor scheme of political thinking, God automatically helped the sons of those who had first helped themselves.) Secondly, he is physically tough; when all his soldiers are sitting under the gazing moon at Agincourt like so many horrid ghosts, it is the king who cheers them:

> For forth he goes and visits all his host
> Bids them goodmorrow with a modest smile
> And calls them brothers, friends and countrymen.
> Upon his royal face there is no note
> How dread an army hath enrounded him.
> Nor doth he dedicate one jot of colour
> Unto the weary and allwatched night
> But freshly looks and overbears attaint
> With cheerful semblance and sweet majesty
> That every wretch, pining and pale before,
> Beholding him, plucks comfort from his looks:
> A largesse universal like the sun
> His liberal eye doth give to every one
> Thawing cold fear, that mean and gentle all
> Behold, as may unworthiness define,
> A little touch of Harry in the night.

He is also courageous in battle and jealous of honour; not quick temperedly jealous like Hotspur, who would

> pluck bright honour from the pale-faced moon
> Or dive into the bottom of the deep
> Where fathom-line could never touch the ground
> And pluck up drowned honour by the locks,

but magnanimously jealous, wishing to share it with his followers. And what a world of difference between the

Hotspur and the cool Hal in this. Hotspur can scarcely book the presence of his own kind on the same battlefield, Henry V wishes no more fellows than he has—indeed reproves the Earl of Westmoreland for wishing them—but ends his famous Crispin speech:

> This story shall the good man tell his son
> And Crispin Crispian shall ne'er go by
> From this day to the ending of the world
> But we in it shall be remembered
> We few, we happy few, we band of brothers,
> For he today that sheds his blood with me
> Shall be my brother; be he ne'er so vile
> This day shall gentle his condition:
> And gentlemen in England now abed
> Shall think themselves accursed they were not here
> And hold their manhoods cheap whiles any speaks
> That fought with us upon St. Crispin's Day.

He is open to entreaty as a civilized being when the field is won; and he gives the glory of his victory all to God.

Altogether he seems a little too good to be true. As Kate, his new French wife does, so we may balk a bit, after the rejection of Falstaff, at such a characterization as he gives himself when wooing her: he is a plain king: he speaks to her plain soldier in 'true English' from a 'good heart'. He is a king, pure and simple. But, as Oscar Wilde would say, Renaissance kings were rarely pure and never simple.

So, by 1599, Shakespeare has taken an orthodox run at history in the *Henry VI—Richard III* tetralogy, he has taken a dramatically more interesting but still philosophically unadventurous run at it in *Richard II,* the two parts of *Henry IV,* and *Henry V.*

But do people always turn out for the best? Do all whores have, like Doll Tearsheet, hearts of gold? Do all thieves have, like Poins, their own honour? Are all subjects as docile and patriotic as Bates and Williams, the latter of whom says, 'For we know enough, if we know we are the king's subjects'?

The answer to all these questions is no, and by 1599 Shakespeare knew that it was, despite the strength with which he had put the opposite case in *Henry V* and in the plays leading up to it. In fact he makes it clear that all the skill of a Henry V cannot, in itself, make history bend to his will. Despite his luck in battle, his fortune in love and the even temper of his subjects, he has to pass on his heritage. And in the last chorus of *Henry V,* Shakespeare says:

> Thus far, with rough and all-unable pen,
> Our bending author has pursued the story,
> In little room confining mighty men,
> Mangling by starts the full course of their glory
> Small time, but in that small most greatly lived
> This star of England: Fortune made his sword;
> By which the world's best garden he achieved,
> And of it left his son imperial lord.
> Henry the Sixth, in infant bands crown'd King
> Of France and England, did this king succeed,
> Whose state so many had the managing,
> That they lost France and made his England bleed.

In other words, the practical business of politics—what we would today call the ongoing tradition—cannot be so simple as Henry VI would like it, or as capable of manipulation as Henry IV or Henry V would have us believe.

Moreover, there are hard things in these history plays. If you believe in degree, as Shakespeare did, the belief sometimes bends the facts. The great speech by the Archbishop of Canterbury about the honey-bees,

> Creatures that by a rule in nature teach
> The act of order to a peopled kingdom,

is spoken *after* he has made it clear to the Bishop of Ely that the King must fight in France so that the religious orders will not lose their property—a not very compellingly Christian view, nor one which puts God very clearly at the top of a legal pyramid. Henry seems very easily convinced that the Salic law does not extend to France. And, finally, Scroop, Cambridge and Grey have to be sentenced to death as traitors before the youth of England can get their mettle aboard for France.

Obviously there is more in the governance of people than the theoreticians would have had Shakespeare believe. The neat and tidy chain of being, with its various degrees, cannot explain everything. Nor can the divine right of kings.

By 1599, therefore, Shakespeare is ready to have a more searching look at the nature of politics, of government and monarchy. Machiavelli had done his work well and the time for a re-assessment of outworn attitudes was ripe.

Shakespeare had to face the fact, if he was to write about government, that people are not always docile and willing to be governed. They are also easy prey to the man who will promise them a lot without knowing how to deliver it. And insurrection caused by demagogues does not always fade away—kings have sometimes been toppled by it, and we have seen four empires dissolved by it in the last twenty years.

As Machiavelli says:

> For touching men, we may say this in general, they are unthankful, unconstant, dissemblers, they avoid dangers, and are covetous of gain; and whilest thou doest them good they are wholly thine; their blood, their fortunes, lives and children are at thy service, as is said before, when the danger is remote; but when it approaches, they revolt.

So says Machiavelli further on:

> A prince . . . cannot observe all these things, for which men are held good; he being often forced, for the maintenance of his state, to do contrary to his faith,

charity, humanity and religion; and therefore it be-
hooves him to have a mind so disposed as to turn and
take the advantage of all winds and fortunes: and as
formerly I said, not to forsake the good, while he can;
but to know how to make use of the evil upon necessity.

Shakespeare knew all this, and the Tudors had proved it.
Henry VII's handling of the Perkin Warbeck and other
revolts; Henry VIII's dealings with the Pope and the Pilgrimage of Grace, Elizabeth's conduct in her religious settlement,
and the ill-fated Northern rising under Northumberland,
where the poor had been executed and the rich fined, were
all examples of actions by princes who were, as all the Tudors
were (except poor dear Mary) Foxes as well as Lions.

There had been some of this in the *Henry IV* trilogy:
John of Lancaster's treacherous method of winning a battle
without fighting, Henry IV's ruminations on his getting of
the throne and, of course, Hal's treatment of Falstaff. But it
was dangerous to do more of this so close to home.

Besides, Holinshed was pretty thoroughly mined already.
Another land, and other leaders must be found to give these
nagging matters a local habitation and a name.

Satirists have nearly always set their attacks on society in
faraway places and times long time ago. Chaucer, in order
to have his say about the Church, had even put one convent
chaplain in a henhouse; Sir Thomas More had talked about
Utopia. Where would Shakespeare's meditations fit?

Rome was the obvious place. Why? Because in Elizabethan
times Roman history was the great place in which to interpret
political motives and movements. Roman history had all
that scholarship needed for its research: there was a large
body of it; it was written in an arcane language; there were
standard authors and recognized sources to go to; and all
the speculation was about people who had been dead for over
a thousand years.

There was another thing, too. To the Elizabethans, Rome had been a place of civil war and shattering internal faction very like the Wars of the Roses. There was a thrill of recognition as Shakespeare and his comtemporaries read their North's Plutarch—a recognition which T. J. B. Spencer has beautifully documented. Writing in the tenth annual *Shakespeare Survey*, he says (and I quote at length):

> Books on Roman history are useful evidence for the normal attitude to the Romans and their story in Shakespeare's lifetime. For it is not so much what we can find in Plutarch, but what Shakespeare noticed in Plutarch that we need to know; not merely Plutarch's narrative, but the preconceptions with which his biographies could be read by a lively modern mind about the turn of the seventeenth century; for
>
> > men may construe things after their fashion
> > Clean from the purpose of the things themselves.
>
> It is by no means certain that we, by the unaided light of reason and mid-twentieth-century assumptions, will always be able to notice the things to which Shakespeare was sensitive.
>
> First then, the title of William Fulbecke's book is worth attention: *An Historicall Collection of the Continuall Factions, Tumults, and Massacres of the Romans and Italians during the space of one hundred and twentie yeares next before the peaceable Empire of Augustus Caesar.* There is not much of the majesty of the Roman People (which Dennis desiderated) in these continual factions, tumults and massacres. In his preface Fulbecke writes:
>
> > The use of this historie is threefold; first the revealing of the mischiefes of discord and civill discention. . . . Secondly the opening of the cause hereof, which is nothing else but ambition, for out of this seed groweth a whole harvest of evils. Thirdly the declaring of the remedie, which is by humble estimation of our selves, by living well, not by lurking well; by conversing

in the light of the common weale with equals, not by complotting in darke conventicles against superiors.

Equally tendentious is what we read on the title-page of the translation of Appian as *An Auncient Historie and exquisite Chronicle of the Romanes Warres, both Civile and Foren in* 1578,

> In the which is declared:
> Their greedy desire to conquere others.
> Their mortall malice to destroy themselves.
> Their seeking of matters to make warre abroad.
> Their picking of quarels to fall out at home.
> All the degrees of Sedition, and all the effects of
> Ambition.
> A firme determination of Fate, thorowe all the
> changes of Fortune.
> And finally, an evident demonstration, That peoples
> rule must give place, and Princes power prevayle.

This kind of material (the ordinary stuff of Roman history in the sixteenth century) does not lend itself to chatter about the majesty of the Roman people. In fact, the kind of classical dignity which we associate perhaps with Addison's *Cato* or Kemble's impersonation of Coriolanus is not to be taken for granted in Shakespeare's time. The beginning of Virgil's *Aeneid,* with its simple yet sonorous *arma virumque cano,* might by us be taken as expressive of Roman dignity. Richard Stanyhurst, however, in his translation of Virgil in 1582 rendered it:

Now manhood and garboyles I chaunt. . . .

'Garboyles', it will be remembered, was Antony's favourite word to describe the military and political exploits of Fulvia.

So revolution, the thought which motivate it, the successful manipulation of the people who are persuaded to indulge in it, and particularly the control of it by its instigators, are surely the theme of *Julius Caesar*—a theme arrived at after a long apprenticeship by a man who is fascinated by the whole question and a man who, with all respect to Dr. Tillyard, was not so much a prisoner of orthodox thinking about

> degree, priority, and place,
> Insisture, course, proportion, season, form,
> Office, and custom, in all line of order,

as he may seem from the history plays.

This makes *Julius Caesar* a real turning point in Shakespeare's work. From the popular and propagandist view of history, conceived in popular and patriotic terms, clothed in pageantry, enlivened with the swirl of battle and jollified with fat old knights, cranky gardeners and funny Welshmen, he moves into a quiet contemplation of what's behind it all. It is as if, up to 1600 he has been impressed with royalty, but that after 1600 he probes behind the pomp and finds the personality. For after *Julius Caesar* his greatest creations are kings or heirs apparent: Lear, Hamlet, Macbeth, and the theme is killing the king. What had been merely a heinous crime for Richard III, a crime in the public good for King John, an event salved by prior deposition in *Richard II*, now becomes the theme for intense and serious probing in *Julius Caesar*.

For what happens in Caesar is a new dimension in Shakespeare. Let us look at it in three movements: what happens to Caesar, what happens to Brutus, what happens to Rome.

At the beginning of the play Caesar is returning in triumph over Pompey. In the history plays, and within the context of Holinshed and Hall, it would be right and proper for the acknowledged head of the state to crush rebellion. For if we leave the Tudor ideology aside, the kings who fought through the Wars of the Roses to put down their turbulent nobles had no more right to assume sole power than Caesar had. And no less—that's why it would be proper to assume that an English Caesar would have crushed an English Pompey to acclaim. But as Caesar returns, two public officials berate the mob for praising him, and in one of the most powerful pieces of rhetoric in the play Marullus belittles Caesar, praises Pompey and shows the fickleness of the people:

> See whe'er their basest mettle be not moved
> They vanish tongue-tied in their guiltiness.

Caesar arrives, is made aware by the soothsayer that there are more things in heaven and earth than may be dreamed of in his philosophy of power. This may be why he flouts the idea of becoming king. The people may want it, he may want it, but there is a collective race-consciousness of fear which amounts to a taboo about this, and he spurns it.

This attitude he is confirmed in. There's something not well with the state, and the signs and portents of Act II underline this. Yet a man who is head of the state must not be affrighted by these—he must proceed. The fact that a Caesar may be stabbed or a President Kennedy shot does not mean that no leader should stir abroad. It is not any misplaced devotion to duty which kills them, it is the psychopathic hatred of lesser men.

So Caesar goes to the Forum and is killed. Why? Because some people fear he may become too powerful. But compare Caesar with Bolingbroke. Caesar gets the plaudits of the people; he crushes rebellion; he will not be fazed by signs and portents; and he exercises power justly and evenly. (He reads the petition dealing with himself last.) Yet Caesar is killed, and Bolingbroke founds a ruling house, and Shakespeare has broken new ground. Because one notices that to a great extent Shakespeare contrives all this. We see Caesar mainly through the eyes of the conspirators, and where Cassius underlines the humanity of Caesar with the scene in Spain and in the Tiber, Shakespeare alters Plutarch and invents the detail himself.

In sum, Shakespeare portrays Caesar as a proper ruler. There is nothing in the play to make him play his part as anything less. But it is through the eyes of the conspirators that we see him. These eyes are different. Cassius and the other conspirators are mainly jealous of him, and angry at the pomp and ceremony with which he surrounds himself. What of Brutus?

The second movement of the play is Brutus. He is the man of honour, of nobility, of inborn greatness, who is, because of this, the arch-conservative. He is averse to killing Caesar, but if tradition demands it, he must act. What was good enough for Brutus's ancestors, who had expelled the Tarquins from Rome, was good enough for Brutus 500 years later. No wonder the *Encyclopedia Britannica*—as opposed to Shakespeare—says: 'The Romans admired him for his respectability, the old-fashioned *gravitas* [yet] . . . he was slow in decision, amazingly obstinate.' So Brutus, rigidly following the old line, is content to murder Caesar (judicially, of course) and explain such an inflammatory act to the populace in the flattest, most pompous, costive language in the whole play.

Thus, Shakespeare, having had Brutus kill Caesar (a heinous fault in Tudor eyes), now shows that such an act, like many other conspiratorial acts done in the name of the people, has no connection with the people. The gulf between noble and base, which Henry V bestraddled for a while, is always there. Brutus is so far to one side of it that he cannot communicate with the other side.

Then—the people. They like Caesar, but are shamed out of their liking by Marullus and Flavius. They respond to Brutus because he is an honourable man and bears that stamp

of nobility which is the mark of leadership even in democratic societies. They are led to reject Brutus by a virtuoso
speaker who plays them as a good fisherman would play a
trout—tickle it, hook it, fight it, exhaust it, then beach it
and live off it.

For in the end the people are at war. And there is no
discipline so rigid to keep the multitude in check as military
discipline, and nothing so calculated to keep those in office
who began it.

Yet there is a curious ambivalence, even ambiguity, in
Shakespeare's treatment of these two latter movements as
themes. Brutus is an arch-conservative, yet he has all the
hesitations, questionings and remorse of a liberal. He is also
shown to be human. Shakespeare is saying that people who
make plots which change the world and who should be able
to govern that part of the world which they take over, are
often better at thinking about it than doing it. As Oxenstjerna
said to his son: 'Do you not know, my son, with what an
infinitesimally small amount of good sense the world is
actually governed?'

And if Brutus is as he is—he quarrels with his lieutenant,
he is queasy about raising campaign money, he makes the
wrong military decision and finally kills himself—what of
Cassius, who has only lust for power to motivate him? And,
particularly, what of Antony who is a political opportunist,
a Machiavellian prince, if ever there was one? Do people
get the government they deserve if these are the governors?

Which leads to the people. As a mob, Shakespeare hates
them. They have greasy caps and stinking breath, are
treacherous, cowardly and stupid. Yet the cobbler is sharp
and can bandy words with the best of them. Perhaps
Shakespeare the dramatist and Shakespeare the man are at
odds. Men and their individuality are the dramatist's stock-
in-trade. Men were more keenly observed by Shakespeare

than by any other writer in history. But Shakespeare the man had seen the prentices rioting in his London; he had seen the ugly face of mindless revolution and he was scared of it. Had he lived later he might have argued for education of the masses. Since he did not, he merely took the only remedy he could see, strong government. That is why, despite his preoccupation with other figures on the way, it is always a Horatio, a Kent or some such solid, down-to-earth character who is left to sort out the mess and get the world back to normal.

In *Julius Caesar* he is moving towards all this, and he has not moved very far. That is why it is such a thoughtful play—why it doesn't answer questions but asks them. That is why it is written in such limpid style. And that is why, I have no doubt, it is so often prescribed for schools. There's a lot in it (and not a jot of bawdiness), and most of it deals with abstract ideas—the ideas of the rule of law.

That may account for two things in its stage history. So abstract and flat is it in its general style, and so one-dimensional are the characters, that it is often hoked up. In 1954, for example, the first two performances noted in the *Shakespeare Quarterly's* annual review of current theatre were 'experiments': the one in Buenos Aires in monologue form; the one at Oxford presenting 'the characters in varying degrees of moral and spiritual corruption'. In 1957 there was a modern-dress production at the National Institute of Health in Bethesda; one in the auditorium of the Unitarian Church in Des Moines, Iowa, which utilized the aisles and the choir loft, and one presented in the ruins of the temples of Bacchus and Jupiter at Baalbek in Lebanon. And in 1955 Jean Renoir directed it in an adaptation in familiar language for the festival at Arles, where it was presented in the old Roman arena, with two hundred and fifty French soldiers as Roman Legionnaires, and fifteen thousand spectators.

I think this is a pity. It is a thoughtful play and should be thoughtfully presented. There is enough action in it for it not to be dull. And there is a second noticeable trend in its stage-history. It is becoming more popular. Now whether this is so because a lot of theatres put on those plays which are prescribed in the high schools and *Julius Caesar* is often so prescribed, or whether it's because Shakespeare's analysis of the politics of revolution has great relevance in an age of revolution, it would be difficult to say.

I hope it is the latter. Because what is going on in Vietnam itself, and the world because of Vietnam; what is happening in Cuba and the Caribbean; what indeed is happening here in Canada between Quebec and the rest of the country, needs a lot of thinking about. And Shakespeare can help us in our thinking both by what he says in *Julius Caesar* and what he raises by inference in our minds.

As Sir Francis Bacon said:

> The images of men's wits and knowledges remain in books exempted from the envy of time and capable of perpetual renovations. Neither are they fitly to be called images because they generate still, and cast their seeds in the minds of others, provoking and causing infinite actions and opinions in succeeding ages; so that, if the invention of the ship was thought so noble, which carrieth riches and commodities from place to place, and consociateth the most remote regions in participation of their fruits; how much more are letters to be magnified, which pass through the vast seas of time and make ages so distant to participate of the wisdom, illuminations and inventions, the one of the other?

And, as Coleridge even more cogently said about poetry:

> [It] prevents men from confining their attention solely, or chiefly, to their own narrow sphere of action, and to their own individual circumstances. By placing them in certain awful relations it merges the individual man

143

in the whole species, and makes it impossible for any one man to think of his future lot, or indeed of his present condition, without at the same time comprising in his view his fellow creatures—we need not wonder that it has pleased Providence that the divine truths of religion should have been revealed to us in the form of poetry; and that at all times poets, not the slaves of any particular sectarian opinions, should have joined to support all those delicate sentiments of the heart (often when they were most opposed to the reigning philosophy of the day) which may be called the feeding streams of religion.

In a sense, I think *Julius Caesar* is such a feeding stream, and though Samuel Johnson found it lacking in vigour and Ben Johnson found it lacking in scholarship, I find it a fascinating play—fascinating both for itself and for the position it occupies in Shakespeare's work, a position which led from the orthodoxies of his youth to the searing, blinding visions of his later days. Without *Julius Caesar* we could not have had *Lear*. And could there be greater justification of any play than that?

August 1965

THE MOOD OF *HENRY IV*, PART 2

John Pettigrew

A teacher of mine once remarked that Dr. Johnson would have been an even greater critic had he sometimes heard a voice from on high calling unto him, 'Samuel! Samuel!' Despite those occasional aberrations to which my teacher alluded—aberrations frequently delightful in their wrong-headed pomposity—Johnson remains indispensable, one of the first men to whom one turns for comment, perhaps above all on Shakespeare. And nowhere is he more impressive and more laudatory than in his comments on the two parts of *Henry IV*:

> None of Shakespeare's plays are more read than the first and second parts of Henry the fourth. Perhaps no author has ever in two plays afforded so much delight. The great events are interesting, for the fate of kingdoms depends upon them; the slighter occurrences are diverting, and, except one or two, sufficiently probable; the incidents are multiplied with wonderful fertility of invention, and the characters diversified with the utmost nicety of discernment, and the profoundest skill in the nature of man.

As the flood of eighteenth-century references to *Henry IV* attests, Johnson speaks not only for himself but for his time.

The nineteenth century, however, found the two plays less to its taste; excessive preoccupation, usually highly sentimental, with Hotspur and even more with Falstaff led to that serious distortion and consequent undervaluing of the plays that persisted well into our own century. As late as 1943, Professor John Dover Wilson, in his admirable book on *The Fortunes of Falstaff*, called *Henry IV* 'a play much neglected by both actors and critics'; indeed it is only in the last twenty-five years or so, years that have witnessed a remarkable and overdue resurgence of interest in all Shakespeare's histories, that Johnson's value judgement has found frequent support. When Kenneth Tynan, for instance, wrote in 1955 that for him 'the two parts of *Henry IV* are the twin summits of Shakespeare's achievement', he was making claims that now find many sympathetic echoes, but that would have been thought highly peculiar not long before.

Neither Dr. Johnson nor Mr. Tynan distinguishes between the merits of the first and second parts: for both men, they are clearly 'twin summits'. So are they for scholars who, like Professors Dover Wilson and Tillyard, have stressed the connections between the plays of Shakespeare's greater historical tetralogy, and have seen the two parts of *Henry IV* as parts of one stupendous whole.[1] It is, however, fair to say that these men are exceptions to a fairly widespread tendency to find the second part inferior to its predecessor, and that Part 2 has not yet generally received its due. To some extent of course, Part 2 is overshadowed by Part 1 simply because most of us don't know it as well. Part 1 is more familiar, and familiarity can breed only increased respect for it. Most school-children are nowadays exposed to Part 1 by their teachers (teachers for whom one's heart bleeds when one considers that they are perennially faced

1 The Stratford Company and its director for the *Henrys*, Mr. Stuart Burge, certainly gave every indication that they shared Johnson's feelings! To see the two parts produced together, as they obviously should be seen to be fully appreciated, was an immensely illuminating experience, and one all the more exciting for those who had seen Mr. Burge's brilliant production of *Richard II* in 1964.

with the appalling task of explaining not only why Falstaff is funny, but that he is funny); again, for every production of Part 2 there are several of Part 1. Then too, we inevitably come to Part 2 with the generally justified assumption that sequels are likely to be inferior works—how many readers know the second parts of *Pamela* or *Pilgrim's Progress*? *Henry IV, Part 2* might well have been more successful had it been called *Falstaff*.[2]

While the greater familiarity of Part 1 and a natural prejudice against sequels are not in themselves sufficient to account for a comparative lack of interest in Part 2, they inevitably serve to condition value judgements on it. What is in fact said by those who do not really admire Part 2? Here are three commentators:

> The Second Part of *Henry IV* is unquestionably inferior to the First Part as a work of dramatic art. . . . [It] is faulty in construction, and occasionally feeble in execution. For the greater part of four acts the poet is occupied with a theme, of which the interest had been exhausted in the previous play, and which grows stale by repetition.

That is the editor of the old Arden edition. Here is the editor of the new Pelican edition:

> Shakespeare found the historical material less tractable than in *The First Part*. Hotspur and Glendower were gone. . . . Among the historical personages there remained the king, Prince Hal, the three other sons of the king, and the principal noblemen of the rival factions. With these Shakespeare does the best that he can.

And, most extreme of the three, here is Richard David, reviewing for the *Shakespeare Survey* the 1951 productions at the English Stratford; after lavishing praise on *Henry IV*,

2 As it was by the Stratford Theatre. Interestingly, Part 2 played to fuller houses than Part 1.

Part 1, he calls Part 2 'that ramshackle rag-bag of a piece . . .
[with] pot-boiler written all over it', and goes on to complain
that Hal has nothing to do, that the rebellion simply peters
out and that the 'nimble comedy' of Part 1 is sadly lacking.
Despite the extremity of Mr. David's view, the comments
of these three critics do essentially reflect the value judgements
of most general readers and, I think, of most critics.[3]

We can see operating here, in men who know Part 2 well,
a prejudice against sequels. Characters, locations, structural
patterns and leading themes are of course carried over from
the first part to the second; the assumption is made that
Shakespeare is trying, vainly, to repeat an earlier success. It
is said that the attempt to repeat himself shows in the structural
resemblances of the two plays, Hal for instance having to
redeem himself all over again. Hotspur, by whose 'light /
Did all the chivalry of England move / To do brave acts', is
dead, and the excitement he gave the rebel cause is lacking
in Part 2. And, the indictment continues, the lack of energy
in the new rebels is only one example of a similar lack of
energy in the play as a whole. Falstaff is not as funny, and thus
Shakespeare is forced to lavish attention on such 'sideshows'
as Doll, Pistol and Shallow to compensate. And they appear,
the Pelican editor feels, in scenes that modern readers may
well find 'tasteless'. In short, the buoyant energy and zest,
the sparkle and gaiety of Part 1 are gone: Shakespeare cannot
succeed in recalling the Muse of Fire that in Part 1 had so
obviously kindled his creative imagination.

Now, the premises of hostile criticism are largely correct:

3 They do not of course reflect the views of all critics! Recent writers
on Part 2 have tended to stress the play's sombreness. My lecture is
especially indebted to the explicit and implicit challenges to conventional views in two illuminating essays: Professor Clifford Leech's
in 'The Unity of *2 Henry IV*', in *Shakespeare Survey*, 6, 16–24; and
Professor L. C. Knights's in 'Time's Subjects: The Sonnets and *King
Henry IV, Part II*', in his *Some Shakespearean Themes*, 45–64.

Part 2's structure does parallel Part 1's; it is a comparatively actionless play; the new rebels lack Hotspur's glamour and energy; Falstaff isn't as funny; some scenes are 'tasteless'; the fire of Part 1 is largely extinguished. But while the premises are correct, the conclusions are not. Shakespeare is not given to repeating himself and he did not try to repeat himself in Part 2. Criticism is bedevilled by those who approach works of art with fixed ideas, and of the bedevilment much criticism of *Henry IV*, Part 2 provides a good example. We have only to clear our minds of pre-conceptions about the kind of play that *Henry IV*, Part 2 might have been to see it as it really is: a work of art which reflects a strikingly different vision, which is conceived in strikingly different terms, from its predecessor. Part 2 is different from, not inferior to, Part 1. Those respects in which it is less grand than Part 1 are not manifestations of flagging energy and inspiration, but, as Professor Leech has stressed, of the different mood that dominates Part 2 and that serves to pull into a new kind of unity the apparently disparate materials of which it is composed.[4]

The first part of *Henry IV* is on the whole a play pleasant, written in a major key; the second part on the whole a play unpleasant, written in a minor key. Part 1 is a play of youth, Part 2 a play of age; Part 1, to use Vernon's words of Hal, is 'as full of spirit as the month of May', Part 2 is a play of autumn or winter. While the continued characters are recognizably the same, their outlooks, attitudes and circumstances are frequently different, less attractive; the new characters, from anything remotely resembling a moral point of view, are not exactly an admirable bunch, and the

---

4 Criticism of *Henry IV*, Part 2 has also been bedevilled by that ridiculous, but surprisingly prevalent, error of confusing quality of subject matter with literary quality. As with *Troilus and Cressida*, the frequent sordidness of Part 2's subject matter is still made the basis for hostile criticism.

more obviously comic ones, Pistol and Doll for instance, appear in scenes that are, altogether appropriately, 'tasteless'. The sordid, the sombre, the bitter—these are part of the fabric of Part 1, but they tend to be buried beneath a flood of high spirits, dazzling gallantry and pure humour. In Part 2 they predominate: we are faced with low spirits, abysmal treachery and a kind of humour that is seldom pure and almost never simple. I do not wish to suggest for a moment that Part 2 does not possess humour in abundance —anyone who is not frequently and profoundly amused by it must be, like John of Lancaster, a cold-blooded person whom one cannot make laugh. Falstaff can be Falstaff still, and he is surrounded by a wonderfully varied group of nitwits. Carried over from Part 1 are the far-from-articulate Bardolph and the interminably loquacious Mistress Quickly, that close relative of Juliet's nurse and ancestor of Mrs. Malaprop; among the new characters who come to life in Part 2 are that delightfully vulgar trollop, Doll Tearsheet; Ancient Pistol, the would-be actor whose only language has been picked up, hopelessly garbled, from the Elizabethan playhouse; Justice Shallow, the epitome of senile nincompoopery, and his companion, Master Silence, a character whom Hudson finely called a 'stupendous platitude', and in whom Professor Knights has noted 'the exquisite lack of positive presence'. These characters, and the raw, rude, rustic recruits are intensely funny. But—and it's a very big 'but' indeed—the humour associated with them has often a nasty bite and leaves a bitter taste. We laugh often, only to be pulled up short by our recognition that the humour is fused with the pathetic, the grotesque, the horrible, to produce responses infinitely more complex than those involved in Part 1.

For one example of the kind of humour of which I am speaking, a very gentle example, I invite you to consider the audience's reaction to Poins's famous line: 'Is it not strange that desire should so many years outlive performance?'— one notes that the initial broad guffaws give way to a kind of laughter involving a note of rueful recognition. Obviously much harsher is the humour surrounding Doll Tearsheet: she is sentimental but not sentimentalized, she spreads humour—and disease. And what of Ancient Pistol, whose obvious grotesqueness is stressed all the more if one accepts the suggestion that he is an ironic recreation of Hotspur in, for instance, his extravagance, his rodomontade, his 'romantic' gestures—it is not, I suggest, accidental that his motto (ending with '*sperato me contento*') reminds us of Hotspur's '*Esperance ma conforte*'—I think great artistic advantage could be drawn from doubling the roles in production. Again, I would instance the undertones to the first scene in which we meet Justice Shallow, a scene in which the 'comic relief' is characteristically Shakespearian with its insistent emphasis on death and mutability, and which involves our uneasy recognition, even while we laugh at Shallow, that the King's justice in Gloucestershire is not in the best hands. For a final example of the quality of the humour, I would ask you to consider one of those ridiculous recruits, Feeble, for it is with him that Shakespeare produces one of those magnificent moments that are so characteristic of him. Feeble is contemptible in appearance, a woman's tailor, an obvious butt. But from another point of view, he is also an admirably brave and patriotic man, and when he gives his great speech our laughter at the recruits' absurdities should suddenly be stilled. Feeble will not grease Bardolph's palm to escape service:

> By my troth, I care not. A man can die but once. We owe God a death. I'll ne'er bear a base mind. An't be my destiny, so. An't be not, so. No man is too good to serve's prince. And let it go which way it will, he that dies this year is quit for the next.

Significantly, his 'We owe God a death' echoes Hal's rebuke to Falstaff before Shrewsbury, 'Thou owest God a death.' Feeble fumbles for words, but his heart is sound; to this apparent imbecile Shakespeare gives the only heroic words in the play, and for once even Bardolph is touched by them. If we are tempted—and we should not be—to see only the funny side of Falstaff's recruiting, Feeble helps us to resist the temptation.

The quality of the humour in the two parts of *Henry IV* is very different. A similar distinction exists in the quality of the parallel scenes in the two parts where Shakespeare's principle is clearly not imitation but transmutation; the parallels are parallels with a difference, and serve to emphasize the sordidness of so much of Part 2 by throwing it into greater relief. How much richer, for instance, is the pathos and agony of the Eastcheap scene in the second part in which Falstaff's drink-befuddled wit cannot extricate him from ridicule when our minds carry us back to the good-natured hilarity of the first part's Eastcheap scene when his wit was so triumphant. How much more ominous, in the same scene, is the knocking on the door when we recall Hal's 'I do, I will' and the ominous knocking that followed that foreshadowing of Falstaff's banishment in Part 1. How different, thanks to Feeble, is our response to Falstaff's recruiting activities in Part 2 (in Part 1, the recruits are anonymous and we tend to see them through Falstaff's eyes). How much more clearly we understand the spirit in which the rebellion of Part 2 is conceived, conducted and concluded, when we contrast it with the spirit of Hotspur's rising. Professor Clifford Leech is surely right when he suggests in his penetrating article on 'The Unity of *2 Henry IV*' that 'the interplay of feelings in this Second Part is so complex that our sympathy resides securely nowhere,' right when he relates the play in spirit to the dark comedies, and right when he says that Shakespeare is here in 'a state of dubiety concerning basic assumptions in the great historical scheme', and that he 'weighs his characters more carefully and questions even the accurancy of his balance'. *Henry IV*, Part 2 is a complex, disturbing and bitter play; Shakespeare's vision had deepened between the writing of the two parts.

That Part 2 is to be very different in mood from Part 1, Shakespeare takes great care to tell us dramatically in the induction and first scene. Johnson complained that the information given in Rumour's induction was 'useless', and he was right if one considers only the facts presented by Rumour. The speech is, however, tonally important, creating as it does a sense of confusion and helping to establish the feeling for a world in which nothing is but what is not, initiating the references to disease that permeate the play, striking a note of contempt for the populace (later to be echoed by the Archbishop of York). The unpleasantness, the sense of confusion, is carried into the first scene with Lord Bardolph's false information and our reintroduction to Northumberland whom we have seen before as the 'haught insulting man', the brutal hatchet-man, of *Richard II,* the 'crafty-sick' coward who betrayed in turn King Richard, King Henry and his own son. As one of the most odious characters in Shakespeare, it is entirely appropriate that he should act as major prologue to set the tone of *Henry IV,* Part 2, as he does above all in a speech that reminds us of Lear, though it hasn't of course Lear's power:

> Let heaven kiss earth! Now let not Nature's hand
> Keep the wild flood confined! Let order die!
> And let this world no longer be a stage
> To feed contention in a lingering act.
> But let one spirit of the first-born Cain
> Reign in all bosoms, that, each heart being set
> On bloody courses, the rude scene may end,
> And darkness be the burier of the dead!

No more than in the past is Northumberland set on bloody courses that threaten his own destruction—the descrepancy between his words and his deeds reflects similar discrepancies in those of other characters in the play; he will shortly commit the last of his betrayals—though only one of many in the play—and abandon the rebels by skulking off to Scotland. And among the new rebels there is no Hotspur to claim that his absence gives a larger dare to their great enterprise.

The rebels of Part 2 are a seedy lot, their rebellion touched with none of the grandeur that, largely because of Hotspur's dynamic qualities, fired the rebellion of Part 1. This rebellion is kindled fearfully without enthusiasm, smoulders fleetingly without hope, and splutters out ingloriously in treachery. Shakespeare stresses the hopelessness of the petty enterprise in the first scene in which we see the rebel leaders together. Mowbray is full of doubts about it, Hastings (the most optimistic of the group) suggests that they can succeed only with Northumberland's aid, Lord Bardolph fears the buds of rebellion will be soon frostbitten. Throughout the scene the rebels seem to be trying to cheer themselves up, trying to convince themselves that rebellion is possible. The Archbishop's decision to proceed against Henry is, moreover, irrational: it in no way follows from the arguments presented, and seems prompted more by disgust at the condition of the times than by anything else, 'Past and to come seems best; things present worst.' It is perhaps Hastings's remark at the very end of the scene that best captures the spirit in which the futile rebellion begins: 'We are time's subjects, and time bids be gone.' Throughout the rebels' scenes we have the sense of men feeling that they are in fact powerless to decide their own fates: time and the times seem to them to shape their destiny. In their own small way the rebels have reached, when we first see them that state of resignation to the inevitable that so many tragic figures reach late on their road to destruction. Yet, despite their fatalistic resignation to the inevitable consequences of a chain of events that they can no longer control, tragic heroes like Macbeth and Hamlet go down fighting. There is nothing of this spirit in the rebels. Their fatalism goes too deep, they appear to be more apathetic than resigned, so that they seem almost to accept as their motto the dying Hotspur's statement that 'Thought's the slave of life, and life time's fool.' When Westmoreland asks York why he goes to war, the Archbishop replies:

> We are all diseased,
> And with our surfeiting and wanton hours
> Have brought ourselves into a burning fever
> And we must bleed for it.

He adds:

> We see which way the stream of time doth run,
> And are enforced from our most quiet there
> By the rough torrent of occasion.

To Lancaster, he later remarks:

> The time misordered doth, in common sense,
> Crowd us and crush us to this monstrous form,
> To hold our safety up.

If, in rebelling, the Archbishop of York and his companions are simply victims of the conditions of the times, they are further the victims (as the rebellion peters out with a whimper of futility) of an atrocious piece of treachery, so appaling and so blatant that John Masefield found it the most terrible thing in Shakespeare. Certainly nothing in the two parts of *Henry IV* is more sordid, though Northumberland's betrayal of his son and Worcester's decision not to tell Hotspur of the King's generous offer before Shrewsbury have something of the same nastiness about them. Neither Worcester nor Northumberland, however, has the bad grace to gloat over his villainy (one notes the heavy conscious irony with which

Westmoreland and Lancaster precede their perfidy: 'My love to ye / Shall show itself more openly hereafter'; 'I trust, lords, we shall lie to-night together'), and neither has the nerve to credit God with his actions as Lancaster does. The treachery is of a piece with the whole sorry and sordid rebellion:

> Most shallowly did you these arms commence,
> Fondly brought here and foolishly sent hence.

Lancaster's remark to the Archbishop is just, and that it is so helps to make even more obvious the sharp contrast with the kind of heroism and reach for honour that animate, in part at least, the rebellion of Part 1. And in that contrast are reflected clearly the profoundly different moods of the two parts of *Henry IV*.

Had it been Shakespeare's intention to create another play with the excitement and energy of Part 1, had he been attempting to repeat himself, it would have been easy for the creator of Hotspur to give a romantic cast to the rebellion without doing any more violence to historical fact that he did in creating Hotspur. He could have endowed, say, Mowbray, with some of the stature he gave Hotspur, could easily have given him a real personality by making use of the fact that this Mowbray is the son of Bolingbroke's opponent at the beginning of *Richard II*. He chose not to do so. Shakespeare also chose not to develop something that could have given a measure of personal force and conviction to the Archbishop: the enmity between the house of Lancaster and the Archbishop's family, the Scroops. This Scroop, the 'gentle' Archbishop of York, so fearful in his brief appearance in Part 1, leads this rebellion, and there is something grotesque in his appearance in armour—churchmen ought not to lead rebellions as the Archbishop realizes and Westmoreland points out. Shakespeare deliberately resists the temptation to give the Archbishop individual reality or force; instead he makes him repeatedly insist, not on the private, but on the public, nature of his cause. Morton tells us that the Archbishop

> Turns insurrection to religion.
> Supposed sincere and holy in his thoughts,
> He's followed both with body and with mind,
> And doth enlarge his rising with the blood
> Of fair King Richard, scraped from Pomfret stones;
> Derives from heaven his quarrel and his cause;
> Tells them he doth bestride a bleeding land,
> Gasping for life under great Bolingbroke.

Richard's ghost continues to haunt Bolinbroke, and the rebels, in Shakespeare's handling of them, tend to become representative figures rather than individuals, representatives of the sickness in the diseased kingdom that was the inevitable consequence of Richard's murder. The force of Carlisle's prophecy near the end of *Richard II* is felt much more intensely in Part 2 than in Part 1 of *Henry IV*.

In reflecting the virtual wasteland that England has become, the atmosphere generated by the rebel scenes contributes to that bitterness of mood that characterizes Part 2. The same mood pervades the court. Before we see the King, we have been told of his sickness, and when we first see him, his decline from the day of Shrewsbury is very marked. Like another king-killer, he has murdered sleep; like the Archbishop, his is obsessed with the diseased kingdom:

> The body of our kingdom
> How foul it is, what rank diseases grow,
> And with what danger, near the heart of it.

To Warwick's remonstrances that things are not as bad as he thinks, he pays no attention, but gives vent to a terrible dispair that has no parallel in feeling in Part 1:

O God! That one might read the book of fate,
And see the revolution of the times
Make mountains level, and the continent,
Weary of solid firmness, melt itself
Into the sea! And, other times to see
The beachy girdle of the ocean
Too wide for Nepture's hips, how chances mock,
And changes fill the cup of alteration
With divers liquors! O, if this were seen,
The happiest youth, viewing his progress through,
What perils past, what crosses to ensue,
Would shut the book, and sit him down and die.

Henry goes on to recall the past, and to paraphrase Richard's prophecy: 'The time will come that foul sin, gathering head, / Shall break into corruption,' a prophecy which he sees now as all too acurate.

In Part 1, Henry's head rested uneasy beneath his crown, but he was nevertheless a commanding figure in his dealings with the rebels, powerful and authoritative in speech, every inch a King. Now he is old and close to death. His sorrow over his son's apparent profligacy weighed upon him in Part 1, but weighs the more strongly here the closer he approaches death, for the sense of paternal sorrow is not only deeper here, but is broadened to include grief for the sufferings that his loved England will endure under Henry V:

                                    My grief
Stretches itself beyond the hour of death.
The blood weeps from my heart when I do shape
In forms imaginary the unguided days
And rotten times that you shall look upon
When I am sleeping with my ancestors.
For when his headstrong riot hath no curb,
When rage and hot blood are his counsellors,
When means and lavish manners meet together,
O, with what wings shall his affections fly
Towards fronting peril and opposed decay!

Henry's fears for the future find their finest and fullest expression in his vision of the appalling anarchy that will follow his death:

> Harry the Fifth is crowned. Up, vanity!
> Down, royal state! All you sage counsellors, hence!
> And to the English court assemble now,
> From every region, apes of idleness!

The Archbishop has been able to say that things present seem worst, past and future best, but there is no such consolation for Bolingbroke, no rest for his perturbed spirit. The present is agony, the future provides visions of even greater horror and the past and Richard II haunt him as he looks back on his usurpation and its consequences. To the King, Shakespeare gives some of his finest verse and creates an ineffably poignant portrait of suffering. Bolingbroke does not approach the tragic, but the pathos is all the more intense if one thinks back to the noble warrior who made his first entrance near the beginning of *Richard II*. Bolingbroke, for me at least, is not the 'vile politician' that Hotspur and many actors and readers have found him to be. He says, and I believe him, that necessity so bowed the state that he and greatness were compelled to kiss; he is for me the man elevated to a kingship he never really wanted, almost without being aware of it, the creature rather than the creator of circumstances, the victim of Northumberland's reach for power and Richard's insistence on giving it up. Whatever his motives in *Richard II,* however, the punishment for his act of usurpation is full and terrible, and one is glad that his suffering is relieved in that very wonderful scene in which the two Harrys are finally, completely and movingly reconciled. The main impression we have of the King in the second part of *Henry IV* is, however, of a man whom Time past, Time present and Time future combine to make another of Time's subjects. Like the rebels, Henry seems no longer capable of positive action, his mood like theirs is one of anguished and despairing resignation to the condition of the times. And when Time bids him be gone, it chooses with a last ironic twist that he shall die in the chamber, not the city, called Jerusalem.

As in other Shakespeare plays, *Hamlet* and *Macbeth* for instance, and as in many legends and myths, the evil and sickness at the heart of things, the King, permeates through the whole land. It is reflected in the references to disease, corruption, time, age and death that run through the whole play. Manifestations of the disorder at the centre of the realm are found of course in the rebel camp, and in the tavern and Gloucestershire scenes in which Falstaff is usually the dominant figure.

Much has been said and written of the differences between the Falstaffs and Parts 1 and 2, and many critics, including great ones, have in the past suggested that Shakespeare's imagination ran away with him in the Falstaff of Part 1 to such an extent that, to make the rejection of Falstaff more palatable, Shakespeare had in Part 2 to cut him down to size —if one may use so unfortunate a metaphor of the fattest part in the two plays. Such views will not now, I think, find any support. Falstaff is different because Part 2 as a whole is different. The Falstaff of Part 1 would tear Part 2 asunder; he would be as much out of place in the weary diseased world of Part 2 as he would be at Agincourt. In Part 2, Shakespeare focuses on the seamier side of Falstaff, but there is no need for an exhaustive discussion of the rather different Falstaff we now see. I wish only to make a few points by way of illustrating the manner in which the different Falstaff is in key with the spirit of the whole play.

We notice in his first scene that, like Henry IV, he is older, and that he is sick. His waddle has become a hobble—he is suffering from gout and the pox. The consequences of his actions and the inevitable ravages of time are catching up with him. In Part 1, Hal had asked him what the devil he had to do with the time of day, and, as many critics have pointed out, Hal's question is a good one: as they have said, the Falstaff of Part 1 lives in an atmosphere of perfect freedom from limitations, including those of time. Falstaff, remark Professors Brooks and Heilman,

> has properly nothing to do with the world of time. He transcends the time-ridden world of important affairs— the world of appointments to be kept, of tasks to be performed, of responsibilities to be undertaken. Time does not exist in his world. . . . In it, one is not dogged by time, just as the child is not dogged by time in his world.

The comment is exact on the Falstaff of Part 1, but it obviously has no relevance to the Falstaff of Part 2. Falstaff now is dogged by time. In Part 1, he often adopted the pose of youth; in Part 2, he tries it only once, in the opening scene with the Lord Chief Justice. And to his pose, the Justice replies:

> Do you set down your name in the scroll of youth, that are written down with all the characters of age? Have you not a moist eye? A dry hand? A yellow cheek? A white beard? A decreasing leg? An increasing belly? Is not your voice broken? Your wind short? Your chin double? Your wit single? And every part about you blasted with antiquity? And will you yet call yourself young?

It's quite a catalogue! Falstaff gets off a remarkably good reply, but never again does he even pretend to be young. And there are quiet and poignant moments with Doll when the pathos of the old man's situation is focused for us, the moment for instance when Doll asks him when he will begin to patch up his old body for heaven, and Falstaff replies: 'Peace good Doll! Do not speak like a death's-head; do not bid me remember mine end.' He himself realizes something of the cruel absurdity of desire's outliving performance when he laments as Doll kisses him, 'I am old, I am old.' (In one of our century's great poems, J. Alfred Prufrock, old in heart, obsessed by time, recognizes that he is almost ridiculous, almost the Fool, and goes on to say, 'I grow old . . . I grow old . . .'; beside that line, I am told, Mr. Eliot wrote in his own copy of the poem, 'Falstaff'. The allusion is not exact, but the affinity of mood is clear enough.) We are told by the drawers that Falstaff once was very angry when Hal referred to his age. In the rejection speech Hal returns to the theme: 'I know thee not, old man'—do our minds carry us back to 'I know you all'?

> I know thee not, old man. Fall to thy prayers.
> How ill white hairs become a fool and jester!
> I have long dreamed of such a kind of man,
> So surfeit-swelled, so old and so profane.

Falstaff is bidden to remember his end; Hal thrusts his age at him as if it were something for which he is responsible. Falstaff cannot escape from old age, nor does he any longer exist in an atmosphere of perfect freedom. In Part 1, his escapades, his fun, had for the most part no serious consequences, his anarchy was relatively harmless. But here we are reminded again and again of the results of Falstaff's lawlessness on Mistress Quickly, on his page, on his recruits, on himself. Moreover, instead of joking for its own sake, Falstaff has now become the schemer, the calculator, the pike in search of dace.

Falstaff is not amusing in Part 2 as in Part 1; his unyoked humour seems frequently to lay an egg. There are would-be jokes in his dialogue with the Justice that don't come off; indeed Falstaff, Lord of Misrule, is clearly frightened of

Gascoigne, Lord Chief Justice. The man who, in Part 1, had a magnificent alacrity in evading charges against him, begins by pleading deafness in his scene with the Justice. He cannot in the one scene that he has with Hal before the rejection evade Hal's charges, and Hal is most emphatically not amused by Falstaff's claim that he dispraised Hal before the wicked that the wicked might not fall in love with him. The joke doesn't work, unlike the similar one after Gadshill. And in his repeated words, 'No abuse', one sees that Falstaff knows all too clearly that his wit cannot now extricate him from any situation. In no scene is the ultimate banishment more clearly foreshadowed. Hal's 'Falstaff, good night' marks the end of their close acquaintance. In the scene, Hal's contempt for the old man is clear, and because we do not elsewhere see them together, it is inevitable that Falstaff's wit must deteriorate. Falstaff needs to match wits with an intelligence equal to his own. In Part 2, he doesn't have it, and it becomes true in a way that villainous company is the ruin of him. To some extent he can act as his own straight man, but with none of his associates can he now carry on a conversation, not with Prince John or Bardolph or Doll, still less with Mistress Quickly or Shallow or Silence. Judged by the company he now keeps, Falstaff's descent is very marked. He is uncomfortable in that company—one notes in the scenes with Shallow and Silence, for instance, how uneasy he is; it is almost pathetic that he should think at one time of the fun he *will* provide for Hal later. He does not enjoy Gloucester. Nor does he enjoy the tavern, which in Part 1 had been a centre of relatively harmless fun, and (despite a brief intrusion by Mistress Quickly) the nearest thing to heaven a man ever knows: a haven for bachelors with wine and song, but no women. The tavern is now a brothel, Falstaff's lechery (only referred to in Part 1) is now openly displayed, Doll and Pistol kill a man in it.

We note further that Falstaff is increasingly the butt. 'Men of all sorts take a pride to gird at me,' he remarks, and it is more true than he means it to be. In Part 1 we laughed with him more than at him, we recognized the force of his comments that hit at Hotspur's philosophy and pretensions; in Part 2, he is increasingly himself the object of ridicule, and he cannot puncture the Justice's philosophy. And when, drunk with hubris, he hears of the death of Henry IV and deludes himself into believing that the laws of England are at his commandment, we come close to despising him for being so blind to a future which we foresee clearly, and do despise him for what he has become. And so he rides off to London to meet Hal and his destiny.

And what of Hal? Johnson insisted, and it is now generally agreed, that Hal is the hero of both parts of the play, Part 1 moving towards a display of chivalry representing a happy mean between the extremes of Hotspur and Falstaff, Part 2 moving towards acceptance of the rule of Law and rejection of Anarchy. To some extent, Hal is caught up in the mood of the play and helps to intensify the feeling of world-weariness. His first line, 'Before God, I am exceeding weary,' reveals a Hal in very different mood from the young warrior's at Shrewsbury. He is disgusted with himself—'Doth it not show vilely in me to desire small beer'—and he takes out his self-disgust on Poins. His record of profligacy is catching up with him: he cannot even lament his father's illness, as he wishes to do, lest he be accused of hypocrisy. The gaiety that Hal showed in the Gadshill episode has gone; we have now a restless, unhappy young man, conscious that his past actions are making his present intolerable, conscious that he has wasted time and that it is now wasting him: 'We play the fools with the time, and the spirits of the wise sit in the clouds and mock us.' Despite his genuine concern for his father's illness, he is to endure a tremendous rebuke from his father, the justice of which he cannot but acknowledge.

Yet if in one sense, Hal's uneasy and unhappy apathy contribute to the dominant mood of the play, that mood in turn is something against which his reformation can appear more goodly. It is he who stands as the redeeming figure in the wasteland, he who in some measure redeems the time as he certainly redeems his father. As Part 2 ends, it is clear that anarchy and vice have been banished, and that the rule of Law has been reasserted in Hal's acceptance of the Chief Justice as his new father.

Nevertheless the ending of the play is not a happy one, for the last few minutes of the action raise questions that are not resolved. The rejection of Falstaff is one of the most discussed things in Shakespeare criticism; rightly so, since the scene is one of the most powerful and complex that Shakespeare ever wrote. It is sometimes grossly oversimplified. It will not do on the one hand simply to say (as was often said in the days of sentimentally-viewed Falstaffs) that Hal is a brutal, heartless prig who casts off the fun-loving man who has ridden all night just to see his beloved Hal—Falstaff's appearance after the coronation, as he himself stresses, has been very carefully staged to create just the right impression of his loyalty and devotion, and we need (as Professor Dover Wilson reminded us) to remember that it is not the Falstaff of Part 1 but the Falstaff of Part 2 that is banished. On the other hand, it will not do either to go to the other extreme from the sentimental and to see Henry's rejection of Falstaff as an entirely laudable action. With all his faults, we still love Falstaff and we must yearn therefore when we see him rejected in summary fashion —were we purely rational creatures we could accept the rejection intellectually without qualms, since we are not, our hearts must to some extent go out to him. We can admire the King for acting as he does, but not the man. Nowhere has Shakespeare dramatized more obviously that gulf between the private and public bodies of the king which so clearly fascinated him. Henry V is Shakespeare's perfect King, but as Mr. Edinborough reminded us, he is not the perfect man; he deserves that awful epithet that A. C. Bradley gave him: 'efficient'. Indeed—the irony is horrible—the perfect King must sacrifice much of his humanity to be the perfect King, as Hal sacrifices it in banishing Falstaff. The rejection is at the same time necessary and inevitable, noble and desirable, disgusting and treacherous.

That Shakespeare meant us to see the end of the action as something other than a conventional comic resolution is conclusively shown by a weak ending that is given, not to Henry V or the Lord Chief Justice, but to, of all people, the treacherous 'victor' of Gaultree Forest. Dr. Johnson complained: 'I fancy every reader, when he ends this play, cries out with Desdemona, O most lame and impotent conclusion.' But Shakespeare does not give concluding speeches to minor figures without reason; Johnson's complaint is unjustified when the conclusion is seen in relation to everything that has preceded it. Prince John tells us that he likes 'this fair proceeding of the king's'. As Professor Leech has remarked, it is not good to be praised by men like John of Lancaster, a man who doubtless regarded his action at Gaultree Forest also as a fair proceeding. John tells us that Hal 'hath intent his wonted followers / Shall all be very well provided for'. I do not think I am being fanciful in suggesting that I would not care to be 'very well provided for' by John of Lancaster; the statement from his mouth conjures up for me visions of thumbscrews and gibbets. The play ends on the note of uneasiness that has pervaded it.

The two parts of *Henry IV* provide Shakespeare's broadest, though not his deepest, picture of life, and there is general agreement that they mark the opening of his greatest period. In nothing is his infinite variety shown more clearly than in the shift of tone he accomplishes between the two parts. We may of course decide that we prefer the exuberance of Part 1 to the sombreness of Part 2, but whatever the respective merits of the two plays, there can I think be no doubt that the second part is more profound, mature and searching. No other sixteenth-century play of Shakespeare marks so major a step on his march to the heights of *Troilus and Cressida* and the great tragedies. It, and not *Julius Caesar,* as Mr. Edinborough so wrongly remarked yesterday, is the play that signposts the way to *King Lear.*

August 1965

KING HENRY IV

Muriel C. Bradbrook

We have heard from Mr. Edinborough that *Julius Caesar* is a questing, probing play of politically disturbing character, reflecting the troubled mood of Queen Elizabeth's last years, and from Mr. Pettigrew that *Henry IV*, Part 2 is also a questing, 'dark' play, and that both point forward to *King Lear,* which (according to Mr. Maynard Mack) is a play of such deeply disturbing force that few can bear to look at it directly. I find myself in agreement with this reading, yet hopefully approaching the possibility of linking both parts of *Henry IV*.

There was once a summer school at the other Stratford where in two successive hours, a first speaker said that anyone who doubted the unity of the great continuous ten-act play was disqualified to understand Shakespeare; while a second said that anyone who thought *Henry IV,* Part 2 more than a feeble 'encore' must be illiterate. The link that I would see is that of adaptability, the imaginative ability to create a part and to play it. In Part 1, this playful, heroic, or sometimes merely crafty capacity distinguishes each of the main characters. In the second part, the role-taking (to use familiar jargon) is subtle, Machiavellian and by no means subjected to plain ethical judgements of right and wrong. In dismissing Falstaff, Henry V appears both kingly *and* treacherous— because his two roles can no longer be played by the same man; the King cannot be true to the reveller of Eastcheap. In the play as a whole, the width of reference and ambiguity of response shows Shakespeare's full maturity. 'The solution to the problem of life is seen in the vanishing of this problem,' said the philosopher Wittgenstein; and Machiavelli's contribution to political thought consisted in dropping theories of political government and observing the facts of behaviour, in all their awkward complexity. 'We are much beholden to Machiavelli', said Bacon, 'who openly and unfeignedly declares . . . what men do, and not what they ought to do.' A famous book on princely education, Elyot's *Book of the Governor,* had aimed in the early sixteenth century at producing a traditionally good, well-equipped and high-principled ruler. Machiavelli perceived the emergence of secular sovereignty; and the rest of the world was horrified at what he saw. It had already arrived when Warwick the Kingmaker, in Henry VI's reign, putting pressure on the Vatican to back his policy, manoeuvred in a way any modern student of politics would readily define; but the next century still had no words for it. Behaviour was ahead of statement, for it is the artist that first catches the implications of behaviour. *Henry IV,* Part 2 came out shortly after the first edition of Bacon's essays; these men, however different their minds, were observing the same phenomenon. Shakespeare gave it imaginative form, Bacon gave it definition.

As an actor, Shakespeare was gifted with a special insight into the quick-change aspects of political life; Protean variety, which was the outstanding quality of Elizabethan acting, elicits exactly what the new politics demanded of the ruler. Many have noted that Richard III is a natural actor in his wooing of Anne and in his scenes with Clarence and Edward. However, he is drawn as conventionally wicked, for 'men should be what they seem.' In *Henry IV,* Shakespeare is questioning the popular frame of assumptions more radically, yet he had to avoid shocking his audience.

The uncertainties, the troubles, the doubtful roles, the lack of any suitable heir—these issues were calculated to touch powerfully the feelings and engage the interest of any audience in the late fifteen-nineties. And the glorious resolution of all doubts in the triumphant coronation of Henry V was exactly what the country was momentarily to feel, when James I peaceably succeeded in 1603. Alas! James was no Plantagenet—but instead of leading his people to war against France, he at least united them to Scotland.

Shakespeare was not writing a political treatise or constructing an allegory, but he was playing variations on a live political issue; in these plays the whole of society enters into the conflict. The colourless citizens of *Richard III,* the symbolic gardeners, Welsh tribesmen, the groom of the stable who appear in *Richard II,* play minor roles. But here the life of London and Gloucestershire and the North is fully drawn into the play, while Shakespeare presents, in ever varying forms, a generous and yet sceptical questioning of that traditional principle which his earlier plays assume. This is political drama in a far profounder way than its dynastic interests would suggest, for the psychology of political life is here developed; the most successful man is he who can adapt himself most flexibly while retaining a clear sense of direction and purpose. This was exactly what the apparently changeable but really determined Elizabeth had done. Unlike her successor, she did not theorize; but she was a superb practitioner.

The Queen *was* the government; so throughout her reign the question of what would happen if she died untimely had troubled her subjects. A disputed succession meant the possibility of civil war—the ultimate worst thing for the sixteenth century (as perhaps it still is). This was a topic which no writer would dare directly to treat on the stage, for the consequences would have been extremely serious; but in the mirror of history it had been reflected ever since the young lawyers in 1561 put on *Gorboduc,* a play written by one of the Queen's gravest counsellors. This play enjoyed a great and continuing success; it is about the wickedness of dividing a kingdom—as Hotspur and the conspirators propose to do. Other plays dealt with similar subjects—*Horestes, Locrine, The Misfortunes of Arthur.* These are now little more than names in a textbook; but then they were the means by which the warnings and counsels of her subjects might be tendered to the Queen herself. They were played before her; when later still in 1601 Essex and his friends wanted to raise the City of London, they put on the old play of *Richard II.*[1] We see this use of history today in such plays as Brecht's *Galileo,* Eliot's *Murder in the Cathedral,* Sartre's *Lucifer and the Lord.*

Within the first part of *Henry IV,* each character plays several roles, and the leading characters often substitute for each other. Falstaff is the father of Hal's wit, the King, father of his chivalry; Harry Monmouth is the son of Henry's loins, but Harry Hotspur the son of his wishes.[2]

Falstaff plays any and every part. His imagination devises ever-fresh fancies for himself and his followers, which are taken up and discarded as fast as they are conceived. He describes Hal and himself as thieves, in gorgeously poetic terms; he next promotes himself to judge—but is ready to turn hangman; he then becomes melancholy and repents. In the heat of exploit Falstaff is a 'young man' that 'must live', and the victim of Hal's love charm; in the next scene he is 'poor old Jack'. Having justified himself for robbery on the grounds of a vocation for it, he raises a tempest of rage when his pocket is picked and takes the opportunity to repudiate

1 The deposition scene was left out of the first printed version and may not, even now, be shown in Ethiopia.
2 'Hal' is a more vulgar abbreviation and is used only in Eastcheap: 'Young Harry' is the familiar form at Court. Compare Falstaff's description of himself: 'Jack Falstaff with my familiars, John with my brothers and sisters, and Sir John with all Europe.'

all his debts. Playing the knight of chivalry, he asks Hal to bestride him if he is down, and boasts that his deeds surpass Turk Gregory's. He rises in fact from his mummer's sham death to claim the spoils of victory.

Against Falstaff's instinctive mobility, Hal's role-taking looks deliberate. He early casts himself for the role of Percy, playing it in a mixture of admiration and irony; in his Revels, he plays the part of Prodigal Prince, with Falstaff as his father; and then, assuming the King, deposes and banishes Falstaff as later he will do in earnest. But he can play the pot-boy in a leather apron equally well. The fantasy life of Eastcheap (even the robbery is a jest), playing at capital crime, at exhortation, at soldiering, is sharply dismissed by the prince, even while he enjoys it. It is Idleness—according to Puritan opponents, the capital sin of all players. Idleness and Vanity are keywords in Part 1; both were favourite terms of abuse for the players, but Shakespeare draws their sting. It is in the comedy of Gadshill, sweeping along through the first two acts, that the grand genial theme of Robbery is stated. Thief . . . hangman . . . gallows . . .: the sinister possibilities are suggested only to be brushed aside, for the thieves are in company with 'nobility and tranquility, burgomasters and great oneyers'. In the older plays, it is the King's own money which is taken. Later the note is graver; the rebels carve up the Commonwealth and use her as their booty; the King himself is confessedly one who stole the diadem and put it in his pocket; the tussle with Hotspur over the prisoners is an attempt at Gadshill measures. According to Holinshed, Hotspur said of Mortimer, 'Behold, the heir of the realm is robbed of his right, and yet the robber with his own will not redeem him.'

Falstaff of Gadshill is succeeded by Captain Falstaff, robbing under royal warrant by his misuse of the King's Press. At Shrewsbury the Prince robs Hotspur of all his honours, and finally, most shameless of all, Falstaff robs the Prince of the glory of killing Percy, and staggers off, a porter of the 'luggage' that once was the fiery Hotspur. The Prince, with an indifference more telling than contempt, offers to 'gild' what he at the same time labels as a 'lie'.

Falstaff's chief weapon is neither his sword nor his bottle of sack, but his jests; his power to defend the indefensible springs partly from nimble wits and partly from that innocent and unstudied shamelessness which breeds lies gross, open and palpable as the fantasies of childhood. Somewhere in Falstaff lurks the small boy who boasts that he has just killed a lion. Only by degrees does he penetrate from his Castle of Misrule, the Boar's Head Tavern, to the world of heroic action in which Percy moves; only in the second part to the world of judgement, organization, political theory which surrounds the King. He is an Actor, not in the calculating fashion of Richard III, but with the instinctive, ductile mobility of a jester who takes up any position you throw him, and holds it.

Henry IV, as in the play of *Richard II,* stands for the life of judgement against that of the fantasy and imagination; it is his superior skill in deploying his forces that defeats the dash and fire of Hotspur.

Percy's scornful mimicry of the popinjay lord reveals that he, like Hal and Falstaff, lives in the life of the imagination. To think of a plot is enough for him; he can feed on his motto *Esperance*; mappery and closet-war are quite alien to him. Yet when he meets the more primitive imagination of Glendower with its cressets and fiery shapes, its prophecies out of the common lore, Hotspur baits Glendower mercilessly. Glendower is Hotspur's Falstaff.

Before Shakespeare wrote, Hotspur was already a potent name in such common lore. Every member of the audience would have known that old ballad of Douglas and Percy by which Sir Philip Sidney had confessed himself stirred more than with the sound of the trumpet. Hotspur's contempt for ballad mongers is ill-deserved, for they were to keep his fame alive. In *The Battle of Otterburn* a single combat, such as the Prince offers at Shrewsbury, is offered by Douglas to Percy, and the conqueror salutes his gallant foe, as the Prince, laying his royal favours on the mangled face, salutes the dead Hotspur. In the ballad, it is Percy himself who

> leaned on his brand
> And saw the Douglas dee:
> He took the dead man by the hand,
> Saying, Woe is me for thee;
> To have saved thy life, I would have parted with
> My lands for years three;
> For a better man, of heart, nor of hand,
> Was not in all the north country.

The resurrection of Douglas to join the conspirators in this play adds greatly to their potency. Hotspur could so easily have won at Shrewsbury; the battle against odds is a true foretaste of Agincourt—the little troop with its Welsh and Scots contingent, led by one man's courage. Harry learns his role at Agincourt from Hotspur's at Shrewsbury.

Harry Monmouth, the changeling prince, born in the enchanted West, publicly takes up the role of chivalrous knight in Vernon's splendid description of his mounting his horse; and Hotspur cries:

> Come, let me taste my horse,
> Which is to bear me like a thunderbolt
> Against the bosom of the Prince of Wales.

The essence of chivalry is the mounted charge: knights must have horses—and rivals to encounter. The images are cosmic, grand. As Harry says, 'Two stars keep not their motion in one sphere.' The image of the rising sun dispelling clouds, which the Prince uses in his opening soliloquy, is inevitably parodied by Falstaff: 'Shall the blessed sun of heaven prove a micher and eat blackberries? a question not to be asked. Shall the son of England prove a thief and take purses? a question to be asked.'

Harry of Monmouth and Hal of Eastcheap are different roles for the same young man, who had learnt many-sidedness among the pots of ale where Hotspur contempt-uously places him. The opening soliloquy shows the Prince as a passionless manipulator of events, whereas Hotspur is carried away by rage, ardour or mockery. In his presence, calculation fails; his uncle Worcester, the supreme Machia-vellian, gives up schooling him and at the last dupes him. (In his source, Shakespeare could have found that Worcester had in fact been tutor to Hal; a suitable appointment, had he cared to develop it.)

Hal's many parts, however, do not cohere as naturally as do Falstaff's. In Falstaff the contradictions spring from a great natural vitality; they are the fruit of abundance; in his presence, jests alone are plotted. The Prince is nimbly versatile, witty in a biting style and noble in a restrained one; irony and control are his modes, as lustiness and shamelessness are Falstaff's. In wit, they are evenly matched; but Hal dis-penses patronage, and a follower can never be quite a friend. The mixture of apparent intimacy and real insecurity which Falstaff develops at the Boar's Head is like that attained by players with such noble patrons as Southampton or Pem-broke; and the real Boar's Head Tavern was one of the players' winter houses. Falstaff harps constantly on Hal's position as heir apparent, and though he may dare to call him 'cuckoo' and ask, 'Help me to my horse, good king's son,' there is behind the Prince's retort, 'What, shall I be your ostler?' something of the sting that appears in 'I know you all,' with its later, more dramatic sequel, 'I know thee not, old man.'

Falstaff's gross body, his constant and clamorous needs, for sack, for wenches, for a hand to his horse (the Prince can vault into the saddle), makes him helpless at times with the helplessness of the flesh and of old age, which raises its voice in the shrill reproaches of the long-suffering Mistress Quickly. Falstaff needs his wits to live; Hal needs his only to jest and is an extraordinarily ascetic Rioter. In the old plays of the Prodigal Son, an addiction to harlots always characterized the Rioter. In Part 1, Falstaff represents misrule and good cheer rather than riotous life. Dover Wilson noted the many images of food which are applied to him—the most frequent is 'butter'; he 'lards the earth' and is 'as vigilant as a cat to take cream'. Though gross, these images are rich, nourishing, festive.

It is because he inhabits such a mountain of flesh that his wit 'strikes fiery off'. He uses his bulk as a shield to turn reproaches into a jest, and in his extraordinary union of the child, the animal and the criminal, never pursues any single aim, so that all his disabilities serve only to illustrate his freedom. The dexterity with which he extricates himself from danger is a quick and natural response; when he hacks his sword or attempts to cozen, he is always exposed. His confidence in himself is deep, animal, instinctive; in this, he resembles Hotspur. They represent the nobility of instinct, a feckless unthrifty splendour of living which is unknown to the prudent court. Coarseness and violence, the stench of the battlefield and the smell of the stable, cling to Hotspur, who would have his Kate swear like a mosstrooper, and leave modest oaths to citizens' wives. The praise of instinct which Falstaff bestows on himself has some truth in it. He swears commonly and most properly by himself, for out of himself a whole world of living roles is created for himself and others to play.

Henry IV has only one role to play—that of the King.

He has shown courage, and a disregard for conventional restraint and for all the sacred taboos in assuming the crown; as L. C. Knights has observed, he remains the embodiment of the guilt that is inseparable from getting and keeping power. His vision of a united England sets him above his enemies; but against his deep repentance, and that of the Prince in face of his father's 'dear and deep rebuke', is set the mock repentance of Falstaff, couched in the canting whine of the sectaries. Falstaff thus protects himself against the unco' guid by stealing their thunder.

Interplay of character, exchange of roles, melting of mood into mood and free range combine to give Part 1 its 'divine fluidity'. All is lucent, untrammelled in the consequence. The consequences are presented in Part 2.

Here the characters are sharper, clearer, more definite; they do not blend but contrast. Instead of lambent interplay, division or fusion of roles is provided, with clear separation of man and Office. There is more oration and less action; the action belongs to the common people, while the King utters his great soliloquies and Falstaff talks directly to the audience on the virtues of sherris sack.

The embodiment of some of the leading themes appears in the Prologue Rumour, and I was sorry that this Prologue was cut in your production. Morally Rumour embodies the Lie; socially, she represents 'rotten Opinion' or Seeming; politically, the unstable and troublesome times. The rebels are first shown a false image of victory, then a false peace which is prelude to a new conspiracy, and finally a false show of war, when the true grief lies in the king's death. She addresses the audience as her 'household'; it is a slightly malicious opening jest.

The last abortive rebellion of Henry IV's reign is led by the two symbolic figures of Mowbray and York; Mowbray, the son of Bolingbroke's first public challenger, and York; the Prince of the Church who echoes Rumour on the 'still discordant wavering multitude':

> The commonwealth is sick of their own choice: . . .
> An habitation giddy and unsure
> Hath he that buildeth on the vulgar heart.

A religious rising in the North was the only rebellion of Elizabeth's reign: as a boy of five, Shakespeare might have seen the levies marching up against the Catholic earls, the Nevilles and Percys. Perhaps some of his London audience had marched too.

To his King's anxious calculations of his enemies' strength, Warwick, who is Shakespeare's countryman and speaks always with the voice of Truth, replies:

> Rumour doth double, like the voice and echo,
> The number of the feared.

Like voice and echo, opposed rulers of church and state recall the deposition and death of Richard II, the Archbishop dwelling on the treachery of the multitude who then denounced and would now worship him, Henry dwelling on the treachery of Northumberland, once Richard's friend, then his, and now his sworn foe.

The connection between ecclesiastical and temporal rule is debated when the armies meet. Lancaster says the Archbishop is misusing his position as God's deputy to take up arms against God's temporal substitute, the anointed King.

> You have ta'en up
> Under the counterfeited zeal of God,
> The subjects of his substitute, my father,
> And both against the peace of heaven and him
> Have here upswarm'd them.

But the treachery of John of Lancaster's ruse is hardly excused by his neat explanation that wrongs will be redressed, while traitors will suffer; and a final blasphemy is not lacking:

> Strike up our drums; pursue the scatter'd stray:
> God, and not we, hath safely fought today.

Comment is provided in the last scene by Henry himself:

> God knows, my son,
> By what bypaths, and indirect crook'd ways
> I met this crown.

No one, least of all Bolingbroke, denies the guilt of usurpation or the conflicts it brings. Treachery in the political sphere replaces the mock robberies of Part 1; the presiding Genius is not Valour but Wit, not Chivalry but Statecraft. God send us His peace, but not the Duke of Lancaster's, the commons might exclaim.

The lament of Hotspur's widow is immediately followed by the appearance of Falstaff's whore; it is one of the telling silent strokes. Doll hangs on Falstaff's neck, and tells him whether she sees him again there is nobody cares. The life of the play resides in these common parts, the roles of his followers who do not think of Hal as their future governor. He himself plays the prentice's part—this was a shrewd touch to endear him to all the prentices in Shakespeare's original audience—an important playgoing group. The action of Falstaff's own followers is largely parody. Pistol presents a great parody of the imaginative life; he outgoes even Falstaff's soaring inventions, a wild impossible creature who talks in scraps of play-speech and feeds on his own mad imagination. If the ghost of Hotspur walks in Part 2, he is named Pistol. It has been said that we always fundamentally talk about ourselves, or aspects of ourselves; so, if Falstaff represents something of Shakespeare's own assessment of himself, may not Pistol be a player's nightmare? A parody of Ned Alleyn's rant, perhaps, but also an embodiment of Shakespeare's deepest fear—a wild tatterdemalion spouter of crazy verses, hopelessly mistaken in all he says and does, thrown off even by Falstaff. Pistol embodies the life of dream, of playmaking at its most distorted and absurd. It is fitting that he brings the deceptive good news of Hal's succession to Falstaff. When the King wakens from his dream of Eastcheap mirth, both Falstaff and Pistol are jailed, Pistol roaring his defiant Spanish tag as he is carried off, in cruel parody of Hotspur's motto, *Esperance*: *'Si fortuna me tormenta, spero me contenta.'*

The great mythological popular scene of the stolen crown is haunted not by an explicit recollection of Richard II, but an echo of his fate, the sad ceremony by which Bolingbroke unkings himself. Giving shape to his imaginary fears, Henry mockingly hails his son, by the new title which for all the audience evoked the 'star of England', victor of Agincourt.

> Harry the Fifth is crowned! Up, Vanity!
> Down, royal state! . . .
> Oh, my poor kingdom, sick with civil blows.

Behind the dying king, the anxious father peers out, as death bores through his castle wall. The man fenced in by Office, the body fretted by care, bequeath themselves to dust. Bolingbroke admits that even his expiatory Crusade had not been without its prudential aspect; he had known only a 'supposed Peace', but he prays for 'true peace' at home in his own son's time. And pat to the catastrophe comes the old prophecy's fulfilment—he is to die in Jerusalem, if not quite the Jerusalem his rather stumbling piety expected.

The transmission of Office, the Demise of the Crown as

distinct from the death of Henry Bolingbroke, involves Prince Henry in the last death-pangs of his old self. In his brief appearance before the King's last sickness, the Prince is shown with Poins, who, unlike Falstaff, is bluntly honest. The prince must mock his own greatness, gird at Poins, but half confide in him. Hal of Eastcheap has no right to weep for a father's sickness, and is well aware of it. He takes up the prentice's part and surveys from this vantage Falstaff's descent 'from a god to a bull'. The encounter is momentary: there is a revival momentarily of the old manner ('Why, thou globe of sinful continents'), a recollection of Gadshill; and a carefully casual goodbye, whose finality was beautifully suggested in the playing on this stage: 'Falstaff, good night.' This is the Prince at his most sensitive, subtle and inconsistent. When he finally takes up the poisoned gold of the crown and receives absolution from his natural father, he becomes warmly and simply a tearful son in the closet; but in public, wearing the 'new and gorgeous garment, majesty', he stands as father to his brothers, son to the Lord Chief Justice and to Falstaff an image of the Last Judgement itself (the Exhortation of the York Judgement Play might serve as parallel to the Rejection speech).

In his fears, Henry Bolingbroke had given a 'character' of his son, in which sharp changes of mood and irreversible decisions are the leading traits. A strong personality, when its deeps are broken up by an internal earthquake, shows a new and unrecognisable landscape. The 'noble change' so coolly predicted in Part 1 is painfully accomplished in Part 2. The Lord Chief Justice, like the Archbishop a symbol of Office, represents the better side of the last reign, all that was true in its 'supposed Peace'. This is how he justifies the jailing of the unreformed Prince:

I then did use the person of your father;
The image of his power lay then in me.

He suggests that Henry should imagine a future son of his own spurning his own image; and the King allows the argument as 'bold, just and impartial'. He is no longer an individual, but a Power whose image may by delegation reside in other bodies than his own, such as those of Judge or Prelate. The shadows of past and future kings melt away as the Sun of England mounts with measured confidence an uncontested throne.

Yet he sets himself under the law: 'You shall be as a father to my youth.' Henry, who had played so many parts, now accepts only one. Complete identification of man and Office closes the visor of his golden armour upon him, and he becomes the centre of the group of brothers, an impersonal Lancastrian King. Henceforth he has an uncontrollable tendency to speak like a royal proclamation. However, in one jest dexterously combining religious reproof and a recollection of old times, Falstaff is symbolically buried:

Leave gormandizing; know the grave doth gape
For thee thrice wider than for other men.

In a metaphor derived perhaps from the parable of the tares, the Archbishop of York had seen the fourth Henry's friends and foes growing so inextricably together that he might not pluck up the one without destroying the other. This is not Henry V's problem in weeding his garden now. Falstaff and that old father antic the law, Justice Shallow, are swept off to prison by Henry's new father and his colder self, John of Lancaster, who, fresh from the beheading of an Archbishop, can hardly see Falstaff's banishment as anything but a 'fair proceeding'.[3] It is a highly conventional scene, the traditional judgement scene for a bitter or moralist comedy, so that even Doll and Mistress Quickly are swept into the net. Rumour is confounded, Seeming is cast off and Order restored.

At the height of his second military triumph, the capture of Colville, Falstaff boasts, 'I have a whole school of tongues in this belly of mine, and not a tongue of them all speaks any word but my name.' This elaborate way of saying that 'Everyone that sees me, knows me,' by its metaphor suddenly clothes Falstaff in the robe which Rumour had worn in the prologue. Within the play he is her chief representative; as indeed he admits by implication in a self-revealing comment on Shallow: 'Lord, lord, how subject we old men are to this vice of lying.'

The delights of the Boar's Head and of Gloucestershire, with their undertones of death and old age sounding through the revelry like the coming of winter in a harvest play, depict the wide Commonwealth, the unthinking multitude of common folk about whom Bolingbroke and the Archbishop have been so loftily eloquent. Among the least of the rout, a little tailor with the 'only man-sized voice in Gloucestershire', suddenly echoes one of Prince Harry's proverbs from Shrewsbury: 'We owe God a death.' Feeble, who outbuys a whole army of Pistols, serves to link the multitude and the throne, as in earlier comical histories such local heroes as George a Greene had done.

The audience feels no compulsion to take the side of law and order; indeed the tragic themes predominate in reading, but on the stage this is Falstaff's play. The imaginative life of the action lies less in the sick fancies, the recollections and foreshadowing of Bolingbroke than in the day dreams

3 No one would dream of calling John of Lancaster 'Jack'.

and old wives' tales of Mistress Quickly and Justice Shallow. Neither Hal nor Falstaff daff the world aside with quite the carelessness they had shown before. More wit and less fun, more dominance and less zest, more shrewdness and less banter belong to these two; humour and gaiety have split off into the life of common men and women. Falstaff's mistaken dream of greatness is shattered and he hears himself reduced to a shadow of the king's imagination; for Henry V stands where his father had stood, for the life of reason and judgement against the life of fantasy.

> I long have dreamed of such a kind of man,
> So surfeit-swelled, so old, and so profane,
> But being awake, I do despise my dream.

This was the formula by which the sovereign arose from a play—'Think all is but a poet's dream,' as Lyly had urged Elizabeth. But against the voice of reason and judgement may be set a feminine voice, which was to be heard again pronouncing Falstaff's epitaph:

> Well, fare thee well; I have known thee these nine-and-twenty years, come peascod time; but an honester and truer-hearted man—well, fare thee well.

Truth resides officially with Henry V, yet in spite of his double triumph (Honour, that 'word', has been snatched from Hotspur as if it were a boxer's belt, and now the Lie and Opinion are banished), Kate Percy and Mistress Quickly remain unconverted; while the incorrigible Pistol produces a line which is both a theological definition of Truth or Constancy and a parody of the motto of Queen Elizabeth herself: '*Semper idem*; for *obsque hoc nihil est.*'

Henry sweeps all the nation behind him, except two women and a few fools. Such exceptions, however, are not to be despised in the world of Shakespeare's England. The uncertainty of the public view of Truth has been demonstrated. 'Thou art a blessed fellow', says Truth's champion, Prince Hal, to Poins, 'to think as every man thinks; never a man's thought in the world keeps the roadway better than thine.' There is no need for an unconditional identification with Falstaff; indeed there is no possibility of it; for the virtue of Shakespeare is to present many incompatibles not reconciled, but harmonized.

August 1965

HENRY V: THE EPIC HERO AS DRAMATIC PROTAGONIST

G. P. V. Akrigg

When Mr. Langham selected *Henry V* for production this summer, he chose a play which, despite its seeming simplicity and directness, poses notable problems for any producer. At the root of these problems lies the fact that Shakespeare himself, writing the play, encountered difficulties which he was not able entirely to resolve. J. H. Walter, in his admirable introduction to the New Arden edition of this play, has indicated why these difficulties arose:

> Shakespeare's task was not merely to extract material for a play from an epic story, but within the physical limits of the stage and within the admittedly inadequate dramatic convention to give the illusion of an epic whole.

This morning I propose first of all to consider the nature of of the epic material which Shakespeare took over from the historians. Then I intend to examine some of the special techniques that Shakespeare employed in his attempt to create an epic drama. Finally I mean to evaluate the degree of his final success or failure.

Behind this play of *Henry V* stands an actual man, the king as history knew him, an authentic hero, the genuine, bona fide article. To say this is not to say that the historical Henry was without fault. Heroes do have their faults even though their worshippers may persuade themselves otherwise. Born in Monmouth in 1387, Henry grew to manhood in an age when a Prince of Wales, once he was of sufficient years, was expected to undertake the government of his principality. He was, in a very literal sense, Prince of Wales. So it happened that Henry, while still in his teens, received a first-class military education in campaigns against Welsh rebels such as Owen Glyn Dŵr (Shakespeare's Glendower). When his father's health began to fail, Henry came to London and took over the direction of affairs in the King's Council. In the half century since Edward III had built up a massive English domain in France, the French had been recovering it bit by bit. Henry, who among his titles had that of Duke of Aquitaine, was convinced that determined military action was the only way to regain the position that England had lost. Unfortunately for him, his ailing father viewed his activities with suspicion and misgivings: he reconstituted the Council and handed over its presidency to the Archbishop of Canterbury, who was committed to a much less aggressive foreign policy.

Retiring from the Council but not returning to Wales, Henry may well have spent part of his time (as Princes of Wales of a certain age are wont to do) in the company of complaisant women and entertaining hangers-on. When Henry's father died in 1413, all such diversions were laid aside. There was, in fact, a distinctly Puritan streak in Henry and his indulgences were probably never very remarkable. He was, moveover, a man with intensely held religious convictions—his surviving letters often strike modern readers as sanctimonious in tone. Henry's most recent biographer, Christopher Hibbert, does not deny that there was much that was priggish and bigoted about him.

As king, Henry lost no time establishing a programme. It contained, quite predictably, the aggressive policy towards France which he had failed to carry while Prince of Wales. Embassies began passing between England and France.

When the French seemed in danger of giving Henry what he wanted, he promptly raised the ante. Henry, in fact, was bent on war and, amid these sham negotiations, was busy raising an army with which to invade France.

Nobody has ever denied that Henry V was a first-class administrator. With remarkable efficiency he and his officers mustered an army of nine thousand excellently equipped soldiers. In August 1415 these troops assembled in invasion ports along the Solent, ready to board the fleet of fifteen hundred little ships which was to convey them to France. The raising of this force had placed a major strain on the financial resources of the country; even the King's plate had been pawned to secure the necessary funds.

At this point we may note that Henry was singularly fortunate in those 'receptivities of the moment' which William James noted as indispensable for the emergence of a hero. The King of France was intermittently insane, the Dauphin was a sickly youth of nineteen, a group of royal dukes divided much of the authority among themselves and the Duke of Burgundy was conducting himself like an independent sovereign. Never was France in worse condition to meet an invader.

Henry's campaign, once he landed in France, soon ran into trouble. He had to capture Harfleur as a base from which to strike inland towards Paris, but unfortunately Harfleur, expertly fortified, well garrisoned and resolutely commanded, held out long past the date that Henry had set for its capture. When the city did capitulate, Henry's army was so ravaged by sickness that, after he had garrisoned Harfleur, he had only about forty-five hundred men (half the number that had sailed from England) to lead inland against the French. So small a force was totally inadequate. When Henry called a council of war, the overwhelming opinion was that he had better head back to England, but to do so, with only one captured city to show for the great expenditures and heavy casualties, and with the nation's high hopes all dashed, would have meant a devastating loss of personal prestige. Henry felt that he could not return home so ingloriously—he must at least have a propaganda victory, if not a real one. Despite the warnings of his captains, he decided to dash northwards through French-held territory and come out at the English stronghold of Calais. What he contemplated was nothing beyond a raid on a grand scale. Henry had his little field army stripped down so that it could travel with the greatest possible speed. He was staking everything on being able to reach Calais before the divided, ill-organized French could learn what he was up to and throw an army into the field to block his line of march. All he wanted was the appearance of a victorious march across France. The real thing, he knew, lay beyond his resources.

And so Henry headed north. However inadequate its numbers, Henry's army at least had the benefit of firm discipline. The King was a man who insisted upon good order. When on this march to Calais one of the English soldiers robbed a church, Henry had the man led bound through the army; then he hanged him from a tree and marched his men in silence past the hanging corpse to make sure they got the point of the exercise. Each evening Henry walked about the camp to make sure that his orders were all being obeyed. He had an interesting device for keeping the English camp from being pestered by the whores who are drawn inevitably to any army. Any harlot who appeared in the vicinity of the camp was warned never again to come within three miles of it. If she did, her left arm was broken. The fact that it was the left arm and not the right might be taken to show the mixture of ruthlessness and mercy which characterized Henry.

While Henry was an outstanding field commander, he was no Napoleon where military strategy was concerned. He was, in fact, consistently out-generalled by the French, right up to the final battle of this campaign. At the very beginning he made a serious mistake. To proceed by the straightest possible route from Harfleur to Calais, Henry had to have command of a ford near the mouth of the Somme. While it is true that he did order the English commander at Calais to send out a force to secure this ford, he started out with no assurance that this operation had been attended to. In fact, to his army's horror, when Henry reached the Somme he found that a French army, moving far more rapidly than he had ever anticipated, was already on the north side of the ford ready to destroy his men if they sought to cross. A more prudent commander might have headed back to Harfleur. Not Henry. Instead he turned east, travelling mile after mile after mile along the south bank of the Somme and finding himself met at every ford or bridge by the French army travelling along the north shore. Conditions grew worse and worse as the half-starved and nearly exhausted English wandered deeper and deeper into the interior of France. At last Henry reached a point where the river swung in a great loop northwards. By a forced march directly east Henry reached an undefended ford ahead of the French and got his army across. But by now an augmented French army, much larger than his own, was ready to interpose itself between him and Calais. Vainly Henry tried to save himself through negotiations. He offered to surrender Harfleur if his army were allowed to march unmolested to Calais. The French, knowing that they held all the winning cards, refused the offer. Finally on 24 October they moved in on Henry, ranging their army directly across his line of march.

The battle was fought on 25 October 1415. And now

luck, which is so helpful to historical heroes, outrageously defied probability and favoured Henry. The French army was at least four times as large as the English, and it had artillery which the English did not. However, there was no French commander-in-chief. Decisions were made mostly by a group of lords with grandiloquent names and picturesque offices, often after heated argument among themselves. The French had forgotten everything they had learned at Crécy, and their battle formation provided an ideal target for the devastating flights of arrows from the English longbows. The French, moreover, had chosen the battle-field unwisely. Two converging lines of woods protected the English flanks, forcing the French cavalry to confine themselves to direct charges which failed because of the stakes the English had driven into the ground. When the French lords advanced on foot, far too many of them, insistent upon being in the place of honour, had jammed into the front rank. As they plodded heavily across the wet grass in their fantastically heavy plate armour, the narrowing front forced them more and more in upon themselves. Coming up to the English lines, the French were so tightly packed that many could not get their arms free to draw their swords. Slipping, many died unwounded, suffocated by the sheer weight of the succeeding armoured lords who fell shoulder high on top of them.

Henry fought that day with the tremendous personal courage which always distinguished him. His English displayed equal valour and at the end, of course, they were victors of the field. But what had really defeated the French was their own lack of command, of direction and of discipline and, most of all, their utter stupidity. Not until Prince Charles Edward left his Highlanders standing defenceless to be exterminated by Cumberland's gunners at Culloden, or until the British generals in World War I sent forward hundreds of thousands to be mown down by German machine-gunners, was the world to see the like of the folly of the French at Agincourt.

What the battle did for Henry's reputation was easily predictable. There is a major principle in such matters. Sidney Hook has usefully defined it in his book on *The Hero in History*:

> There is a natural tendency to associate the leader with the results achieved under his leadership even when these achievements, good or bad, have resulted despite his leadership rather than because of it. Where many factors are at work, the fallacy of *post hoc, ergo propter hoc* has a fatal plausibility to the simple mental economy of the uncritical multitude.

The victory at Agincourt was attributed entirely to the heroism of Henry V, and not to the lunatic tactics of the French. The King's monumental blunder at the mouth of the Somme was utterly forgotten. Back he came to England for a hero's welcome. Nothing succeeds like success, and in 1417, when he returned to France for his Normandy campaign, carrying with him the aura of Agincourt, Caen surrendered without a blow.

Lord Raglan, making survey of the mythic process which marks the emergence of a hero, has seized upon the developing legend of Henry V as the best example of this process to be found in English history. The numerical odds at Agincourt became more and more fantastic with re-telling over the years: not four or five against one, as in fact they were, but at least ten French to each of the English. The English losses became smaller and smaller with successive narrators. Subsidiary episodes attached themselves to the legend: the story of the wildcap boy who miraculously, overnight, became the greatest captain and statesman of his time, and the fiction about the tennis balls and the hero King's splendid reply. National pride thrilled again and again to the name of Agincourt, and Henry was remembered not as the cold calculating gambler who had had luck on his side, but as the great national hero. Just listen to the Tudor historians on the subject of Henry. First, Edward Hall writing about 1542:

> He was the blazing comet and apparent lantern in his days; he was the mirror of Christendom and the glory of his country; he was the flower of kings past, and a glass to them that should succeed. No emperor in magnanimity ever him excelled.

And then Raphael Holinshed writing about 1577:

> A majesty was he that both lived and died a pattern in princehood, a lodestar in honour, and mirror of magnificence: the most highly exalted in his life, the most deeply lamented at his death, and famous to the world alway.

Obviously historians could not be expected to keep up with such a man. A great epic poet was needed fittingly to celebrate his greatness. About 1595 Samuel Daniel, writing his *Civile Wars* (a work that we know Shakespeare perused), presented the ghost of King Henry lamenting that, in the days when he had performed his great deeds, England had had no great poet able to celebrate them in epic poetry:

> O [cries the ghost] what eternal matter here is found!
> Whence new immortal *Iliads* might proceed . . .
> O that our times had had some sacred wight,
> Whose words as happy as our swords had been.

And he expressed the hope that Queen Elizabeth, living in in a golden age of poetry, would detail one of her poets to write the epic that Henry deserved. Daniel plainly had challenged his fellow poets to bend the bow of Ulysses, to show what they could do in the epic line.

And so we come to the late spring or early summer of 1599 when William Shakespeare sat down to write his *Henry V,* making good his promise of several years earlier, at the end of Part 2 of *Henry IV,* to go on with the story of Henry V, 'with Sir John [Falstaff] in it and make you merry with fair Katharine of France'. It is not without significance, by the way, that Shakespeare had waited two years to tackle this final play in the *Henriad.* What probably impelled him to undertake it now was the immediate situation in England. All Ireland had blazed into revolt, and the Earl of Essex, accompanied by his close friend, Shakespeare's patron, the Earl of Southampton, had newly set out with an army of sixteen thousand foot and thirteen hundred horse to re-establish the English authority and bring in the rebel Earl of Tyrone, in the greatest military venture of Elizabeth's reign. Essex's army was larger than that which Henry had taken to Harfleur. Inevitably there was a mood of national and military pride, and Shakespeare deemed the moment right for a stirring war play featuring the great martial hero of the English, a play in which he would not fail to draw 'a lower but loving likelihood' between Henry V and the Earl of Essex.

Did Shakespeare really believe in heroes such as the Henry V of Hall and Holinshed? Perhaps not. A couple of years later, in *Troilus and Cressida,* he was to do a thorough 'debunking' job on the epic heroes of Chapman's Homer. But, even if the thought had occurred to him, he would hardly have dared to give any such treatment to Henry V, the particular darling of the Elizabethans. If Shakespeare had presented the real Henry with all his aspects, including his limitations, his occasional craftiness and slightly nauseating sanctimony, he might have provoked the most notable riot in the history of the Elizabethan theatre.

Shakespeare decided to play it straight. His Henry would

be the traditional hero King. Half borrowing a phrase from Hall, he too identifies his Henry as 'the mirror of all Christian kings'.

And now we come to the question of how Shakespeare sought to make a play do the work of an epic poem. One device he employed was the use of spectacle. He wanted to give his audience great panoramic views of the English invasion fleet, 'a city on the inconstant billows dancing,' of Harfleur wreathed with cannon smoke, of the massed charges of the French chivalry against the little band of English at Agincourt. Unlike some purists, I think Shakespeare would have enjoyed the resources of technicolour and cinerama for such occasions. If they have managed to get a print of Oliver's film up to Heaven, I can imagine Shakespeare in some celestial viewing-room murmuring during the Agincourt sequences, 'Ah, *that's* what I wanted.' Unfortunately, as Ben Jonson had recently pointed out, the Elizabethan playhouse was ludicrously inadequate for the staging of spectacle, especially of battle scenes. Shakespeare, however, was able to provide the spectacle he wanted, using what many will think a better way, tremendously evocative phrases thrown from the prologues into the imaginations of the audience:

> Suppose within the girdle of these walls
> Are now confined two mighty monarchies,
> Whose high upreared and abutting fronts
> The perilous narrow ocean parts asunder.

A prologue is, of course, a narrative not a dramatic device. Shakespeare knew as much, and in that wonderful scene in *A Midsummer Night's Dream* in which he has Bottom propose that Peter Quince write a prologue to bail the little company out of their difficulties with their play, Shakespeare notes how an incompetent playwright will use a prologue as a crutch when his dramaturgical skills are not enough. Nobody, however, has criticized Shakespeare for his superb prologues to *Henry V*. The reason, of course, is that *Henry V* has to be at once a drama and an epic poem. And the prologues help wonderfully to establish the epic dimension, both through what they say and through the superb sustained poetry of the saying.

Another of Shakespeare's techniques—I think Professor Dover Wilson was the first to comment upon it—was quite deliberately to make his play basically a series of tableaux exhibiting Henry as a judicious statesman, Henry as a battle leader, Henry as the brother of his soldiers, and so on.

Allied in part to this 'tableau technique' is the use of extended, formal set speeches quite in the *ipse dixit* manner, speeches such as that of Henry to the Dauphin's ambassador, to his troops before Harfleur, to Montjoy the French herald and to his army on the morning of Agincourt.

Let us pass from epic techniques to epic subject matter. If Shakespeare can hardly provide his hero with a miraculous birth, he at least so elaborates on the theme of sudden reformation as to give him a miraculous rebirth:

> The breath no sooner left his father's body
> But that his wildness, mortified in him,
> Seemed to die too. Yea, at that very moment,
> Consideration like an angel came
> And whipped the offending Adam out of him,
> Leaving his body as a paradise
> To envelop and contain celestial spirits.
> Never was such a sudden scholar made,
> Never came reformation in a flood
> With such a heady currance, scouring faults.

Thus the Archbishop of Canterbury builds Henry up before he ever comes on the stage. And when he does appear, we are given demonstrations of virtue after virtue in this nonpareil among kings. He is devout and respectful, but also incisive in putting the ethical problem of war to the churchmen. He is the thoughtful statesman attending to the protection of England against the weasel Scots. He is magnificently royal in dealing with the effrontery of the miserable French. Everything about Henry is admirable. Thus Shakespeare, quite contrary to historical probability, makes Henry in no way inspired by his father's Machiavellian advice 'to busy giddy minds with foreign quarrels' so as to assure peace at home. On Shakespeare goes, building his Henry up, and up and up.

Just how committed Shakespeare was to the mythic Henry is indicated in his report of the casualties after the battle of Agincourt. Shakespeare has Henry receive a paper showing that ten thousand French lie slain. Then the King receives a second paper giving the number of English dead:

> Edward the Duke of York, the Earl of Suffolk,
> Sir Richard Ketly, Davy Gam, esquire.
> None else of name, and of all other men
> But five and twenty.

Twenty-nine English slain and ten thousand French! This is myth in its naivest form. And Shakespeare knew that it was. For in Holinshed, the quarry from which he got most of the materials for this play, Shakespeare had read:

> Of Englishmen, there died at this battle, Edward duke of York, the earl of Suffolk, Sir Richard Kikelie, and Davie Gamme, esquire, and of all other not above five and twenty persons, as some do report; but other writers of greater credit affirm that there were slain above five or six hundred persons.

Somewhat similarly, though Holinshed supplied him with

the real reason for the plot of Cambridge, Scroop and Grey (a desire to replace Henry with the man who they believed should have received the crown by succession from Richard II), Shakespeare excluded it and with it the suggestion that Henry like his father was a usurper. No, Henry is the perfect hero. Without defect or flaw.

This whole matter of heroes and hero worship is interesting for both the historian and the psychologist. The need of individuals and societies to find heroes when the going gets particularly rough is something which can be studied from a variety of angles. To the Freudians it is all part of the continuing search that some people conduct, even in adult life, to find a parent substitute who can give them the feeling of security that mother and father gave them in infancy. Ability to communicate a sense of security appears to be an essential part of the hero as we find him in history. Other requirements follow as a matter of course. The hero must be self-sufficient, able, as Marshall W. Fishwick has noted in his book on *American Heroes,* to 'turn within himself for the support and solutions he needs'. He must, also, of course, be an activist, with a programme into which he can draw those who turn to him to supplement their own deficiencies.

Sidney Hook, in the book to which I referred earlier, notes three motives which drive men to seek heroes: a need for psychological security; a tendency to seek compensation for personal and material limitations; and a flight from responsibility. Shakespeare was aware of all three of of these, and one of the interesting things about his play is, especially in the scenes just before Agincourt, the exploration he conducts of these social aspects of the hero. We see Henry V functioning as hero in the social sense when we find him giving reassurances, crying that he would not have with him one man more from England to share the honour of the coming victory. Henry likewise gives compensation for the personal and material limitations of his followers:

> We few, we happy few, we band of brothers.
> For he today that sheds his blood with me
> Shall be my brother. Be he ne'er so vile
> This day shall gentle his condition.

Brother to the hero King! What further compensation could be looked for? But then we come to the third motive on the list, the flight from responsibility. And it is here that Henry rises above the hero level. Now devotion to a hero-leader becomes shoddy and morbid when it becomes a device, as so many men have made it, for shedding the individual's personal moral responsibilities. Such hero-worship becomes one of the faces of fascism. And Shakespeare makes Henry a hero of an exceptional kind when he has him refuse to give his followers that release which so many men crave: 'Every subject's duty is the King's, but every subject's soul is his own.'

As Shakespeare worked with his play, there was one particular danger of which he must have been aware: that in producing the epic he would lose the play. The risk lay in that element of impersonality which tends to invest an epic hero. For the epic hero tends to be great and nothing more. He strikes us as a natural force rather than as a human being. Aware of this danger, Shakespeare, once he has given us his opening demonstrations of the greatness of Henry, begins in Act II a series of moves to put us in touch with the man himself, with the human personality behind the royal facade. Accordingly, we are shown Henry in a number of very human situations. We have him as a man suffering agonies at betrayal by his closest friend. There is profound personal tragedy for Henry in Scroop's treachery; it is as if Hamlet had discovered that Horatio had secretly sold out to Claudius:

> What shall I say to thee, Lord Scroop? Thou cruel,
> Ingrateful, savage and inhuman creature!
> Thou that didst bear the key of all my counsels,
> That knew'st the very bottom of my soul,
> That almost mightst have coined me into gold
> Wouldst thou have practiced on me for thy use?

Similarly we have the fine passage in which Henry speaks, though significantly in soliloquy, as a man with the needs of a man, one who knows that Ceremony with all its magnificence cannot give the sleep that the peasant gets, but that the King craves in vain. And then, again in soliloquy, on the very eve of Agincourt, we are shown a terrible gnawing worry in the heart of Henry, one that he has revealed to no man—for a hero must not reveal uncertainty— but that has haunted him all along and now becomes agonizingly intense on the eve of the battle in which he may die. Is he truly the King of England? Or has his father's sin of usurpation been inherited by him, robbing him of all authority to seek the French crown, and charging his soul with the unlawful death of those he had led into this war?

> Not today, O Lord,
> Oh, not today, think not upon the fault
> My father made in compassing the crown!
> I Richard's body have interred new,
> And on it have bestowed more contrite tears
> Than from it issued forcèd drops of blood.
> Five hundred poor I have in yearly pay,
> Who twice a day their withered hands hold up
> Towards Heaven, to pardon blood, and I have built
> Two chantries where the sad and solemn priests
> Sing still for Richard's soul. More will I do,
> Though all that I can do is nothing worth,

Since that my penitence comes after all,
Imploring pardon.

In these lines Shakespeare is fighting hard to make Henry
a living figure for us, to make his play not only epic but
dramatic.

How well has he succeeded? To judge by many of the
critics, not very well. Let us listen to three of them. First
of all, William Hazlitt, one of the great Shakespearian
critics:

> We feel little love or admiration for him. . . . How
> then do we like him? We like him in the play. There
> he is a very amiable monster, a very splendid pageant.
> As we like to gaze at a panther or a young lion in their
> cages in the Tower, and catch a pleasing horror from
> their glistening eyes, their velvet paws, and dreadless
> roar, so we take a very romantic, heroic, patriotic and
> poetical delight in the boasts and feats of our younger
> Harry.

And here is Yeats:

> He is as remorseless and undistinguished as some natural
> force. . . . Shakespeare watched Henry V, not indeed as
> he watched the greater souls in the visionary procession,
> but cheerfully, as one watches some handsome spirited
> horse.

Finally I quote from Mark Van Doren, whose little book
on Shakespeare contains so much good sense and insight.
Van Doren does not liken Henry to a panther, a lion, or a
horse. His verdict is more damning. The great rhetorical
speeches of the king he calls 'the golden throatings of a
hollow god'.

As one additional witness that Shakespeare failed essentially
with *Henry V,* I shall cite the author himself. There is
evidence that Shakespeare had a rough time writing this
play. Right off we have in the prologues the constant

references to the inadequacies of his theatre, not only in the opening prologue but in later ones, as in that to Act V in which the Chorus is still begging the audience

> to admit the excuse
> Of time, of numbers, and due course of things,
> Which cannot in their huge and proper life,
> Be here presented.

I take this continuing restiveness about his theatre as indicative of a certain dissatisfaction with his play.

We may notice, too, that Shakespeare has some trouble getting airborne in the first act. Here we have that long, exceedingly dull speech by Canterbury on the Salic Law as invalid and consequently no bar to Henry's inherited right to the French throne. That speech goes on and on, a most uninspired paraphrase of Holinshed, even preserving uncorrected Holinshed's arithemetical error in computing the time when the Salic Law was first instituted. About the only thing we can do with this speech today is to load it with comic stage business. Some critics have sought to excuse the excessive length of Canterbury's speech by saying that Shakespeare's contemporaries were so litigious themselves that they would have followed with great interest this lengthy argument. I am inclined to dismiss this as humbug. I suspect that Shakespeare, like many another author sitting down to what he knows is a very difficult job, resolutely made his pen start moving, and kept it going on and on with the elementary opening material, while hoping to muster force for a breakthrough. Generally, of course, an author returns to cut and revise an otiose opening section. Was it one of the signs of defeat in Shakespeare that he never pruned Canterbury's speech?

I have noted how, again and again, Shakespeare tries to move in on Henry the man, to make him fully alive and immediate for us, to draw upon our sympathies for him as a man like ourselves. Superb as these passages are, the breakthrough is never really achieved. Or, if it is made, it is made only fitfully. I think it was sheer desperation in this matter that drove Shakespeare at last to that final wooing scene between Henry and Katharine. Few critics have anything good to say about this part of the play. Just recall such passages as that in which Henry tells the fastidious Princess of France: 'If I might buffet for my love, or bound my horse for her favours, I could lay on like a butcher.' As Professor Goddard has remarked, this is the very butchery of love. The most famous of all the indictments directed against this scene is, of course, Dr. Johnson's:

> I know not why Shakespeare now gives the king nearly such a character as he made him ridicule in Percy. This military grossness and unskilfulness in all the softer arts does not suit very well.

Johnson could only decide that 'the poet's matter failed him in the fifth act and he was glad to fill it up with whatever he could get.' I would suggest a somewhat different answer. Shakespeare was not the first Elizabethan to attempt a play on Henry V. There survives an earlier play with which Shakespeare was obviously well acquainted. Entitled *The Famous Victories of Henry V*, it is a primitive thing, tuned to the taste of the groundlings. It ends with a no-nonsense offer of marriage to Katharine by plain English Harry:

> Tush Kate, but tell me in plain terms,
> Canst thou love the King of England?
> I cannot do as these Countries do,
> That spend half their time in wooing:
> Tush wench, I am none such,
> But wilt thou go over to England?

This is, of course, exactly the note of Shakespeare's wooing scene. I would suggest that Shakespeare, sick at his only momentary flashes of success with Henry, at the very end settled for the cheap crude success with the less critical part of his audience that had been achieved by *The Famous Victories*. There follows the passage in which Henry and Burgundy exchange dirty jokes like a couple of horse troopers. That Shakespeare at the end knew that in the light of his own standards he had failed is, I believe, an inescapable conclusion. Remember the words of the Epilogue:

> Thus far with rough [the courting scene was on his
> conscience!] and all unable pen,
> Our bending author hath pursued the story,
> In little room confining mighty men,
> Mangling by starts the full course of their glory.

And now for the final question. Why had Shakespeare failed? Various answers have been suggested. One is that the structure of the play, the prologues, the tableau scenes, the essential absence of dramatic suspense, kept the play from achieving real dramatic movement. I don't think much of this answer myself, believing that the epic devices helped more than they hindered. Professor Dover Wilson says the trouble is that Shakespeare waited too long, had gone too far into the play before beginning the process of humanizing Henry. It could be.

I myself would suggest some other answers. One deals with the very nature of the epic hero. Even in his raw, natural state, before myth has purged him of his faults, a hero is essentially an uninteresting sort of person. Dimension, not complexity, marks the hero. The very simplicity of his character and of his responses, which is a major source of his epic strength, makes him rather unpromising material for a dramatist. An essential part of any such hero, as we have seen, is his self-sufficiency. But does not this very self-sufficiency almost inevitably mean a degree of isolation which can be fatal in the protagonist of a play? I find myself recalling what a reviewer wrote after reading Lindbergh's autobiography, Lindbergh who in 1927 got 3,500,000 letters from admirers telling him he was a hero. The thing that impressed Brendan Gill was how hard it was to get close to Lindbergh as a human being. 'Prodigious reserves of valor, probity, temperateness, and endurance are required of such a man; and the doom of the hero is dreadful, not least because it has so little to do with ordinary human preoccupations, like happiness, and unhappiness.' Shakespeare seems to have had the same experience with his Henry V. Perhaps Shakespeare was attempting an impossible task, and by his very nature the epic hero cannot function as a dramatic hero, or at least as a Shakespearian dramatic protagonist.

There is however a further matter to be considered. Today we recognize hero-worship as essentially a feature of man's immaturity. Max Eastman, writing in Hitler's time a book he teasingly entitled *Heroes I Have Known,* recalled the days of his boyhood worships of the usual heroes, then went on to write:

> I became an adept of that faith which so easily degenerates into the *Führerprinzip.* I know the inner feel of this adolescent psychosis which is sweeping like a deadly epidemic through the world. I know how a growing mind throws it off.

Today surely we do regard hero-worship as something primitive and atavistic. Hero epics after all do really belong to primitive literatures. We know, of course, that we must have leaders and that society cannot function without them. But, if we are mature, we know that our leaders like ourselves will be flawed persons. For those of us who have any claim to sophistication in our thinking and in our experience of life the cult of the hero is, as Eastman says, 'an adolescent psychosis'. I would suggest that we are not ahead of Shakespeare in this. A year or so after *Henry V*, Shakespeare was to write *Hamlet,* a play that he could write with utter conviction and with a complete giving of himself. With it he made perhaps the greatest breakthrough in the history of drama. Recall, I beg you, Hamlet's words: 'I am myself indifferent honest, yet I could accuse me of such things that it were better my mother had not borne me,' and 'Use every man after his desert and who shall 'scape whipping.' We are miles beyond the naivetes of heroes and hero-worshippers here!

In short, I suggest that by 1599 Shakespeare had himself matured to the point where he simply could not believe in the sort of hero that Hall and Holinshed and the rest of them had made out of Henry V. He was incapable of the atavism required to write with complete dedication to his hero. In short, Shakespeare had progressed far far beyond the Elizabethan view of Henry V when he came to put him on the stage. He did the best he could with superb technique and wonderful poetry, but the central conviction was not there and so we have, in Van Doren's phrase, 'the golden throatings of a hollow god'. That is why theatrical history has shown that for *Henry V* really to succeed it needs some special aid—audiences in a patriotic wartime Britain, terrific spectacle, or even a superimposed topical parallel dealing with English- and French-Canadians.

I hope that none of you will think I have come to Mecca to hurl a stone at the Prophet. Generally where Shakespeare is concerned, I have a hard time keeping on this side of idolatry. *Henry V* is in so many ways full of wonderful things—the description of Falstaff's death, Burgundy's superb speech on peace, Henry's anguish at betrayal by his friend, the magnificent poetry in the prologues, all sorts of splendid little touches along the way. One could go on and on. And it all adds up to one thing, a failure of Shakespeare's is more to be prized than the success of a lesser man. 'Failure' and 'success'—what relative words they are! And one of the things most to Shakespeare's credit is his failure with *Henry V*. For here lies an irony. Shakespeare lamented that he could not rise to the concept of the epic hero. The truth is that the very concept of the epic hero is naive, primitive and immature in the modern world. And Shakespeare belongs with the modern world. The trouble was not that he could not rise to the level of the concept of the epic hero, but that he could not descend to it. Shakespeare does some splendid faking in *Henry V*. But his heart, to his credit, was not in the business. He was too far along the road to greater things.

August 1966

WHY NO *HENRY VII*?

(with a postscript on Malvolio's Revenge)

Michael Burn

I am glad (for my own sake only) that Professor L. C. Knights left Stratford yesterday, since this first talk of mine will be running in barefaced defiance of a dictum of his. He wrote, in the well-known essay, 'How Many Children Had Lady Macbeth?', 'The good critic points to something that is actually contained in a work of art, whereas the bad critic points away.' For most of the next hour I intend, with deference, to point away.

I am curious about certain characters Shakespeare seems to have left out, certain voices briefly evoked which he allowed to fall silent. Reading what is now known of the Elizabethan age and thought germinal by everyone, I wonder if his vast tapestry is not after all a little thinly stitched? Where is the Puritan? (We shall come to Malvolio later.) Where is the champion of civil rights and individual liberties, the turbulent hero, barely respectful towards even the Queen, of the nascent House of Commons? Where, at that morning of discovery, any portrait of the explorer, the colonizer, the buccaneer? About the father-figure of those twin creations for which, I take it, England will remain celebrated, Parliament and the British Empire, the swan of Avon seems to have been almost as uninterested as Louis XVI of France about the outbreak of the Revolution.

Ben Jonson, we are told, took Thomas Sutton as his model for Volpone. Heywood wrote a play about Sir Thomas Gresham. But where, in all the works of this son of a

Stratford burgess, the friend of burgesses, a burgess-to-be himself, is any full-length picture in which we can recognize a great English merchant or financier or businessman? Shylock? Surely not. Antonio? We know his private character, and a little about his argosies, but not much. Where are the tradesmen, the apprentices, who appear in hosts in other contemporary playwrights? Where the ambassador, or the civil servant? Shakespeare's age was the original cloak-and-dagger age, but there is no spy in Shakespeare.

Where even, to use a phrase Churchill was using at the age of seven, are the enemies of Albion? During the 1590s, the period we are considering, during which the plays we are watching were composed, England was at war with Spain. But are we to see in either of the Princes of Aragon, whether in *Much Ado* or *The Merchant of Venice,* or in the musty and lovable Armado, that nation which most Englishmen of the day treated as the incarnation of wickedness, cruelty and danger, and still expected year after year off their coasts, brandishing the whips and faggots of the Inquisition? In Shakespeare the enemy is still France.

And Elizabeth herself? At the end of *Henry IV,* Part 2 the Epilogue kneels to pray for her, in a formality found in several plays by others. In *The Merry Wives,* Hobgoblin, the fairy crier, remarks, 'Our radiant Queen hates sluts and sluttery.' She was used to somewhat more lavish tribute than that. In *Henry V,* she is 'our gracious Empress'. She was used to more than that. Dr. Leslie Hotson would have us believe that *Twelfth Night* was first given in her presence, and that for Olivia we should read Elizabeth. As always, one would like to believe him; but can we? How would she have taken those lines we heard the other night? Viola, disguised as Cesario, has arrived on an embassy from Duke Orsino. She asks to see Olivia's face.

OLIVIA: We will draw the curtain and show you the picture.
          . . . Is it not well done?
VIOLA: Excellent well, if God did all.

The Queen could have approved the second answer,

> 'Tis beauty truly blent, whose red and white Nature's
> own sweet and cunning hand laid on,

but how, with her arsenal of paint and Himalayan ginger
wig, would she have responded to the first? And there are
other, more sinister lines, in *King John,* which I shall come
to later. I omit the paean in her praise in *Henry VIII,* since, if
Shakespeare wrote it at all, he wrote it long after she was
dead. Perhaps those few lines in *A Midsummer Night's Dream*
to the 'fair vestal throned by the west . . . the imperial
votaress', perhaps they were enough; and yet they are a very
little puff among the clouds of incense that steamed daily up
to her from Shakespeare's contemporaries.

And what of her Tudor predecessors? There is one of
them, about whose lack of development in the plays I am
especially curious: Henry of Richmond, later King Henry
VII. Shakespeare's first tetralogy, written between (say)
1589 and 1593, ends with Richmond victorious at Bosworth.
For the second he went back in time. Written between 1595
and 1599, it ends with the conquest of France by Henry V
and the King's marriage. Thirteen years later he wrote or
contributed to the writing of *Henry VIII.* When he died he
had thus immortalized the memory of every English
sovereign from the end of the fourteenth century to the
middle of the sixteenth—save one. Henry Tudor, Henry of
Richmond, appears only for an instant as King. He gains the
crown, but loses Shakespeare. Why?

A play on what the chronicler Edward Hall called Henry's
'politic governance' could have found a public, could have
served a purpose, could have been attractive to the author.

The Welsh had become significant, and Shakespeare liked the Welsh. Henry had honoured Shakespeare's forbears on both his father's and his mother's side, and Shakespeare was as avid as anyone for honoured forbears. A play on Henry VII would have offered great scope for prophecies and fanfares at the accession of James I, since James owed his right to the throne, and England and Scotland their uniting, to Henry's foresight in wedding his daughter to the King of Scotland. Most cogent of all, Henry was the Queen's grandfather and the founder of the Tudor dynasty. From him she had inherited a cunning, a curiosity, a caution and a transfixing meanness, avarice and sense of the value of money, on which, especially the last, rested much of her own success and the stability of England in her reign. Francis Bacon likened Henry to those contemporary founders of the French and Spanish monarchies, Louis XI and Ferdinand of Aragon, and called them the Three Magi. I can imagine no more grisly trio to present themselves at a nativity. It is true of all of them that they did destroy the centrifugal power of the great nobles and establish the centralized and necessary structure upon which their successors built. Henry (the least grisly of the trio) made possible the century in which Shakespeare was born and became known. He was the unifier: of England and Wales, through his Welsh blood; of England and Scotland, ultimately, through his daughter's marriage; and of divided England through his own marriage with the heiress of the House of York. He was distant from Shakespeare about the same distance in time, as is today from Sir John A. Macdonald or Abraham Lincoln, whose achievements for Canada and the United States meant, and perhaps still mean, much the same as did his for Elizabethan England. He appears in the final scene of the first tetralogy, not exactly on a white horse—it was the black villain Richard who rode a white horse at Bosworth—but in shining armour, the golden circlet settling on his saviour brow. Now at last could those kindred citizens, who had spent years slaughtering one another, go forward endlessly together as one people. Such was the legend. Such had been in part the truth. And there Shakespeare leaves him, hoping and praying, with scarcely so much as a reference, and certainly no arias, to come.

It is easy to reply that as a laureate he had done his stint with nine patriotic plays in about nine years; or that the framework of real people, real events, real dates in recent history (however much he pulled them about), had become a strait jacket, and that from now on his thronged and headlong imagination could only live unfrontiered and unconfined. This kind of development has occurred in many writers. But it is not an unaccountable miracle nor a law of nature. It is something which has been prepared. It has causes in the writer himself, and in the world he inhabits, and their interaction.

In popular Elizabethan legend and in certain of the chronicles, Henry VII was the king who exorcized the curse. By curse I mean a belief, or superstition, deeply embedded in a nation, or a family, or an individual, that God, through themselves and others, is wreaking vengeance upon them, generation after generation, for some wicked act committed in the past. Perjury will be repaid with perjury. Blood will have blood, and royal blood have rivers. Shakespeare, we all know, traced back the curse to the deposition and murder of Richard II. Not until the end of the first tetralogy had he grasped and subdued the colossal theme he had got hold of. But it is there, right from the beginning, right from Joan of Arc's announcement in the second scene of *Henry VI*, Part 1: 'Assigned am I to be the English scourge.' We need not trace its detailed course. Any writer, even of modest talent, can make something of a curse. If he chances to be a sublime poet, and the curse is royal, and native, and contemporary, he can do anything. You can see Shakespeare, as his consciousness and control over this motif gathers, piling crime upon crime, and almost mathematically requiting them with retribution after retribution, tirelessly elucidating the text Tolstoy set up at the opening of *Anna Karenina,* 'Vengeance is mine. I will repay,' and the dread verse in the Old Testament, 'For the Lord thy God is a jealous God, and will visit the sins of the fathers upon the children, even unto the third and fourth generation.' The sins mount, and the visitations mount, until their all-but-climax in Act IV of *Richard III,* when the three royal women, bereft by murder and their own ambitions of sons, husbands, grandsons, sit down to a dreadful threnody, a stichomythia of desolation, and finally to Bosworth, where the apparently unending thread of blood may seem to have been cut.

It is not to be wondered at that, having come so far, Shakespeare had to go back in history for his sequel. He could not leave such a theme. He had to track it to its source, like someone retracing a great river. *Richard II* is, throughout a kind of mapping of this source.

The grim texts follow one another like flocks of ravens. Every commination is hideously fulfilled. The curse is the chief and continuing rope which binds and is woven by both tetralogies, thin at the outset, growing ever denser as Shakespeare's mastery over words and movement strengthens. Falstaff is not a central C-major theme, but a Gargantuan incidental. Agincourt is the true climax of *Henry V,* but only an episode in the whole saga. Everyone in the audience listening to the English heroics knew that, a few years later, they could as well have been spoken by the French, and had in a sense already had their force and fetch annihilated by Shakespeare himself in the plays already written. The final lines of last night's Chorus were not needed to remind them:

> Henry the Sixth, in infant bands crowned king,
> Of France and England, did this king succeed,
> Whose state so many had the managing
> That they lost France, and made his England bleed,
> Which oft our stage hath shown.

Then indeed might have been the time for a play about Henry VII. Something was needed to reassure people that all had in the end been well, the curse lifted, the ghosts well and truly laid.

But had they been?

On the contrary. There was in Shakespeare's supposedly absolved and liberated sixteenth century, abundant evidence that the curse had, in fact, continued, was not dead in his lifetime and might return even bloodier than before. He had found it, explicit, in the chronicles. To learn what really became of it after the battle of Bosworth, he had only to read on and to follow up certain of his leftover characters. That delicate Princess of France, for example, so beautifully played last night by Diana Leblanc. She married the 'star of England', and within a year had given birth to the boy who became Henry VI. Within four years, she was a widow. A few years later she went to live in open sin with a handsome but obscure Welsh squire called Owen Tudor. The liaison was legalized afterwards as marriage, and she became thereby the grandmother of Henry VII and great-great-grandmother of Elizabeth. Shakespeare does not mention her again. Could it have been because her father, Charles VI of France, was syphilitic-mad, and her son Henry VI sometimes more than a little dotty, and she herself perhaps a carrier of insanity? 'Madness in great ones must not unwatched go.' No, indeed; but it must also not be shown upon the public stage, especially if the great ones happend to be recent forbears of the Queen.

In *Richard III* Shakespeare presents us briefly with a boy

and a girl, the children of the murdered Duke of Clarence; they add to those who have lost sons and husbands those who have lost a father. What became of them? The plays are silent, but history is not. The boy, Edward, Earl of Warwick, survived into youth. To the Yorkists he was the true King, they called him the White Rose. By birth he had a better claim to the throne than Henry VII and was the last Plantagenet in the line of male descent. Henry put him in the Tower, out of harm's way and to prevent him marrying (much as in *Henry IV*, Part I—according to Shakespeare—Henry Bolingbroke kept Edmund Mortimer). Indeed, to unhappy Warwick might have been given the lines which Shakespeare, with far less accuracy, gave to Mortimer, and which sound the prelude to the Wars of the Roses:

[He] hath detained me all my flowering youth
Within a loathsome dungeon, there to pine.

Edward of Warwick pined within the Tower for fourteen years. Only twice did Henry let him out: the first time when Lambert Simnel was impersonating him, to be paraded through the streets of London as living proof that Simnel was an impostor, and the second time to be beheaded. His execution was a judicial murder and put a skeleton in the Tudor cupboard, perhaps their first. Sir Walter Raleigh wrote in the Preface to his *History of the World,* 'The death of the young Earl of Warwick shows that he [Henry VII] held somewhat to the errors of his ancestors'; in other words, like Henry Bolingbroke, like Richard III, like all the rest save Henry VI, he destroyed people who were in his dynasty's way.

The story has even more sardonic and far-spreading undercurrents. For some time Henry VII had been negotiating with Ferdinand of Aragon a treaty against France, which was to be cemented by the marriage of his eldest son Prince

215

Arthur to Ferdinand's daughter Katharine. Bacon, in his history of Henry VII, speaks of a correspondence between the two sovereigns—he may have seen it—in which Ferdinand wrote that the succession to the crown of England remained insecure so long as young Warwick lived, and that he was loth to send his daughter into danger. According to Bacon, although Henry later laid the blame for Warwick's execution on Ferdinand, he himself gained by it 'a sinister fame', and 'did not observe' that it had 'brought a kind of malediction and infausting on the marriage as an ill prognostic'. How ill, I need hardly remind you. Prince Arthur died, and Katharine of Aragon married his brother Henry; years later, when Henry had decided to divorce her, 'she used some words,' Bacon tells us, to the effect that it was God's judgement upon her marriage to Prince Arthur, which had been 'made in blood'—the blood of Warwick.

So much for the little boy in Shakespeare's play. What about the little girl, his sister? She was married off to a wealthy knight, Sir Richard Pole, but continued to be known in her own right as Countess of Salisbury. Katharine of Aragon, perhaps out of guilt for the brother's murder, showed Lady Salisbury special favour. Henry VIII at first treated her with honour and paid for the Italian education of her son Reginald. Katharine (according to her biographer, Professor Mattingly) devised a marriage of atonement between Reginald Pole and her daughter Mary Tudor, which did not come off. He became a brilliant scholar and a devout Roman Catholic. The divorce and separation from Rome separated him from the King. Safe in exile in Europe, he wrote Henry sentences of passionate rebuke, in revenge for for which the King (urged by Thomas Cromwell to root out the last remnants of the Yorkist faction) sent to the block first his brother Lord Montague, and then his mother Lady Salisbury. She was nearly seventy; the story runs that the executioner was a novice, and her head had to be hacked at before it would come off. Fifteen years later, in Mary Tudor's reign, this son Reginald returned as Cardinal, gave the kneeling House of Commons the Papal absolution, and received England back into the Roman Catholic fold; and he had his part, during the holocaust that followed, in sending many Protestant martyrs to the stake.

Such were the fates, not long before Shakespeare's birth, of the two children he introduces so briefly into *Richard III*. In the minds of those most nearly concerned, the boy's murder brought the divorce and the separation from Rome; the girl's son brought the reconciliation with Rome and the fires of Smithfield. To an imaginative, dramatizing mind, they could be seen to represent the two great religious factions which were to divide England for generations.

And what of the direct descendants of Henry VII himself? Several of his children died in infancy. Of those who survived, take his sons first. Arthur died before he could inherit. Henry VIII succeeded, and left a trail of blood. Of his children by Katharine of Aragon, several were still-born or died in infancy. Anne Boleyn was delivered of a still-born child and was beheaded. Jane Seymour died in childbirth. His only legitimate son, Edward VI, died in early youth; so did the bastard he had designed to make his heir. His two surviving daughters, Mary and Elizabeth, came to the throne and both died childless. King Lear invoked Nature to curse Goneril:

> Into her womb convey sterility.
> Dry up in her the organs of increase,
> And from her derogate body never spring
> A babe to honour her!

But what of the sterility of the Tudors?

And the daughters of Henry VII, those who survived to marry into another line? The beautiful Mary married a worn-out lecher of a French king, who died a few weeks later. This merciful event released her to make a secret marriage with her true love, the Duke of Suffolk, for which Henry VIII rewarded them with a colossal fine and the confiscation of their jewelry and plate. Their eldest son died young. Their daughter married the Marquis of Dorset, who was beheaded. Their grandchild was Lady Jane Grey; forced unwilling on to the throne, she reigned for a few days and was beheaded. Margaret Tudor, the second daughter of Henry VII, married James IV of Scotland, who was killed at Flodden. Twenty-eight years later their son, James V, died (it is said, of grief for the defeat at Pinkie), leaving as his heir the infant daughter whom we know as Mary Queen of Scots. Margaret took as her second husband the Earl of Angus, who deserted her; their grandchild was Darnley, who was murdered. She married a third husband, Lord Methven, with whom she was accused of spying for the English by James V, her son.

Death in childbirth, death in infancy, to a degree striking even in an age when of five children born to the aristocracy at least two failed to live out the first year and at least one more died before maturity, death in the promise of youth, death in battle or after battle, murder, sterility, death by execution—such was the descent unto the third and fourth generation of that Henry of Richmond, that Galahad from Anglesey, who appears so shining and so full of hope after Bosworth at the historical conclusion of Shakespeare's two tetralogies. It is carnage. Could anyone seriously pretend that Henry VII had exorcized the tragic past? For any writer who believed in a curse, who had written plays about a curse, if this was not the continuation of a curse, I do not know what more was needed. And Shakespeare knew all this. It was fact. It was part of the active memory of his age. Sir Walter Raleigh wrote no plays; but in his *History,* published in 1616 against the will (and no wonder) of James I, he wrote: 'God is not wearied by the long process of time, nor won to give his blessing in one age to that which he hath cursed in another'; and of Henry VII, by way of illustration, 'His possession in the first line ended in his grandchildren as that of Edward III and Henry IV had done'; and of Henry VIII, 'If all the pictures and patterns of a merciless prince were lost in the world, they might all again be painted to the life out of the story of this king. . . . And in the end . . . it pleased God to take away all his own without increase.'

I am curious whether Shakespeare, for all his adroitness in the manipulation of historic fact, could have circumvented such an appalling catalogue and devised a play about Henry VII acceptable during the lifetime, let alone in the presence, of his granddaughter. Surely the old hideous thunder still hung in the air; and he could no more reject thunder than he could reject the sun.

There is something else relevant to the dramatic treatment of a curse, which recalls something Mr. Michael Langham said at your Seminars in 1961. He remarked on a discovery of Shakespeare's that turned him from a good dramatist into a great one; that 'the outward clashing of character with character is poor dramatic material when compared with the conflict within the fermenting spirit of one man.' The theatrical power of a curse intensifies, not as the cursers multiply it upon the cursed, but as the cursed, within themselves, become aware that it is at work against them and that they are damned in this world, whatever may become of them in the next. You may call the spirit which injects them with this belief Superstition. I prefer to call it Conscience. Throughout the two tetralogies one can watch, simultaneously, the unfolding of the curse and the embodiment of Conscience, materializing like an Arabian genie and growing ever more towering and more relentless. King after king, grand seigneur after grand seigneur, even the commoners and the illiterate, become more deeply stricken as Shakespeare's own awareness of his theme develops. It begins perhaps in an aside of poor honest sincere Henry VI, in Part 3 of his play: 'I know not what to say. My title's weak.' It continues in the grimly comic scene between the two murderers of Clarence; on through Edward IV, learning of the death of Clarence:

> O God! I fear Thy justice will take hold
> On me and you and mine and yours for this!

through Tyrrel after two more assassins have smothered the little princes: 'Hence both are gone with conscience and remorse'; to a climax on the eve of Bosworth, when Conscience brings before sleepless Richard III the accusing phantoms of all those whose blood he has spilt:

> My conscience hath a hundred thousand tongues,
> And every tongue brings in a separate tale,
> And every tale condemns me for a villain . . .
> Guilty, guilty!

Again, can one wonder that Shakespeare, having once grasped this theme, had to go back in time to develop it, like the theme of the curse itself, from its source? Knowledge of guilt for the murder of Richard II becomes the leitmotif of Henry IV. He will not reward his agent Exton: 'The guilt of conscience take thou for thy labour.' He knows he must live the rest of life with it himself:

> **My soul is full of woe**
> **That blood should sprinkle me to make me grow.**

He yearns to set out on pilgrimage, but civil war, his chastisement, prevents him. He too cannot sleep. Already, in *Richard II,* he fears that the wildness of Prince Hal has been sent to punish him. He longs to believe that his heir, regenerate, will wipe out the crime:

> God knows, my son,
> By what by-paths and tortuous crook'd ways
> I met this crown . . .
> To thee it shall descend with better quiet,
> Better opinion.

He recommends Prince Hal to divert men's minds from civil strife with foreign quarrels; but when the Prince, as Henry V, follows this advice, he too must have his mind set at rest by the Archbishop before invading France, lest the curse continue: 'Can I with right and conscience make this claim?' And on the eve of Agincourt he prays desperately (and how well this inner dread has been shown in Mr. Langham's production and Mr. Rain's performance):

> Not to-day, O Lord,
> O not to-day think not upon the fault
> My father got in compassing the crown!

He wins Agincourt and France; but soon his son will lose it all. Remember that the prophecy Shakespeare gave to Exeter:

> Henry born at Monmouth should win all,
> And Henry born at Windsor should lose all,

Shakespeare took from Holinshed, who attributed it to Henry V himself.

Conscience, this major character without a written part, stalks fully formed out of *Henry V* into the non-historical plays which follow. It possesses Lady Macbeth in the sleepwalking scene, and King Lear on the blasted heath:

> Poor naked wretches, whereso'er you are
> That bide the pelting of this furious storm . . .
>   O, I have ta'en
> Too little care of this!

It strikes King Claudius: 'O, my offence is rank, it smells to Heaven,' and stands, of course, at the side of Hamlet:

> I have heard
> That guilty creatures sitting at a play
> Have been struck so to the soul that presently
> They have proclaimed their malefactions . . .
> The play's the thing,
> Wherein I'll catch the conscience of the king.

So much, briefly, for the conscience of imaginary kings and princes in a theatre. What of the Tudors in real life on their real thrones? Henry VII was deeply disturbed about the uncertainty of his right and became more and more pious as he aged. A maddening perverted conscience made sterile Mary Tudor a fanatic, and might, had he lived, have made another of Edward VI. When we think about Elizabeth's conscience, we recall at once the shifts she went to in order to avoid responsibility for the execution of Mary Queen of Scots; how she hinted that Mary might be made away in secret; how, the deed once done, she declared in a fury of self-exculpation that her authority had been abused; and how poor Mr. Secretary Davison found himself her scapegoat, and his career in ruins. Surely into this hysteria there entered a recollection of the curse that had descended on the murderers of Richard II and might now descend on her. She knew about it well enough; she once compared herself to Richard. Is there not an echo in *King John* (IV, iii)? The King has given Hubert the same hints to remove Arthur that Elizabeth sent Sir Amyas Paulet to remove Mary. Hubert returns and allows the King to understand that Arthur is dead, whereupon the King at once declares he never meant it. Listen to some of his lines, written only some seven years after Mary's execution, with Parliament restive and Essex perhaps already planning insurrection:

222

[to Hubert]

> Hadst thou but shook thy head or made a pause . . .
> Deep shame had struck me dumb, made me break off . . .
> But thou didst understand me by my signs . . .
> And consequently thy rude hand to act
> The deed which both our tongues held vile to name.
> Out of my sight, and never see me more!

[to himself]

> My nobles leave me, and my state is brav'd,
> Even at my gates, with ranks of foreign powers.
> Nay, in the body of this fleshly land,
> This kingdom this confine of flesh and blood,
> Hostility and civil tumult reigns
> Between my conscience and my cousin's death.

'My cousin's death'—Elizabeth and Mary were cousins. Does one not guess that, as Shakespeare's audience left the theatre after hearing those lines, one or two at least murmured the Elizabethan equivalent of 'Wasn't that a little near the knuckle?'

At the end of his life Shakespeare wrote or helped to write a play about Henry VIII. We know from history how, seeking justification for the divorce from Katharine of Aragon, Henry hawked his conscience round Europe much as Byron hawked his bleeding heart. In Henry's long speech in Act II, Shakespeare touches the theme with irony. The King has to appear honourable in his own eyes. He will not have a word against Katharine. All the same, he must be honest first with God; and unhappily, he explains, some chance words of a French bishop's about the legality of marriage with his deceased brother's wife

> Shook
> The bosom of my conscience, enter'd me,
> Yea, with a splitting power.

He had been driven to wonder if this might not be the

223

reason he had no male heir. After God, he had to think of
England, and

> Thus hulling in
> The wild sea of my conscience, I did steer
> Towards this remedy [the divorce] . . .
> I mean to say,
> I meant to rectify my conscience.

Lust and Anne Boleyn have nothing to do with it. The
divorce is all for God's and conscience's and England's sakes.
Later in the play Anne is crowned Queen; and when she
crosses the stage, a gentleman in the crowd pays a most
backhanded compliment to the purity of the King's motives:

> Thou has the sweetest face I have ever looked on . . .
> The King has all the Indies in his arms,
> And more and richer, when he strains that lady.
> I cannot blame his conscience.

Such satire upon the scruples of the Tudors could never have
been uttered publicly during Elizabeth's lifetime.

Why no Henry VII? It may be clear by now that what I
am really asking is, why did Shakespeare turn aside from
plays concerning his own epoch? *Henry V,* dated 1599, became his farewell to English history, as *Twelfth Night,* dated a
year or two later, became his 'farewell to mirth'. The ensuing
plays (until *Henry VIII*) are set, if in Britain, centuries ago;
or in ancient Rome; or else are fantasies. The Tudor century,
so assertive and so lavish in achievement, ended upon doubts
that could not be expressed directly on the stage. Victorious
Richmond on the field of Bosworth had prayed:

> God, if Thy will be so,
> Enrich the time to come with smooth-fac'd peace.

At the time those words were written the Tudor line was
already doomed. Retribution had descended to the third

generation; there was and now never could be a fourth. The Queen was barren. The dynasty had lasted a mere century, only thirty years longer than those 'threescore and ten years' which Warwick, in *Henry VI*, Part 3, scorns as

a silly time,
To make prescription for a kingdom's right.

Fears of the Queen's death, which had beset court and nation since her succession, sprang no longer from the risks of marriage and child-bearing, or some sudden illness, or assassination, but ran level with the course of Nature.

> When clouds are seen wise men put on their cloaks.
> When great leaves fall, then winter is at hand.
> When the sun sets, who does not look for night?
> All may be well, but if God sort it so,
> 'Tis more than we deserve, or I expect.

Thus, in *Richard III,* the anxious citizens; it was the voice of many in the dusk of Elizabeth's long day. Any hour that sun might set, that great leaf fall, and who and what would follow her? A new dawn, or civil war again? The history plays of the 1590s are a gigantic and anguished prayer to England not to mar the morning of the seventeenth century with those fatal errors that had made her a battlefield during the fifteenth.

Nought shall make us rue,
If England to herself do rest but true.

God and Sir Robert Cecil did 'sort it so' that the Stuart great-grandson of Richmond's daughter Margaret came bloodlessly to the throne, and then surely might have been the opportunity to celebrate the ending of the curse. Shakespeare did not take it. He was right. Ten years later Henry, the brilliant Prince of Wales, patron of poets, scientists and scholars, died at the age of twenty-two. His brother Charles succeeded him, and was beheaded.

Why no Henry VII? It was a rhetorical question, of course, and an occasion for speculation too. All countries have had their unifiers, and after a time the unification has dissolved, and its dissolution called for someone new. James I was a unifier, in his way; so was William III. Sometimes they come in peace, sometimes in war, and poets often like to write about them. Since the death of Winston Churchill, William Shakespeare is, I suppose, once again the greatest living Englishman. Writing at the beginning of our Empire he warned us then, and seems (now that our Empire is at an end) to warn those who have succeeded to our power, that the most brilliant promise, the most ebullient energy, inventiveness and self-confidence, are also attended by terrible anxieties. For his warnings, for his hopes, for his wisdom, how can we ever cease to be grateful to him?

A Postscript on Malvolio's Revenge:

Yesterday I spoke entirely in the poetic terms of the curse, and it seems right that we should speak in those terms first, Shakespeare having been one who imagined poetically, created poetically, and as a poet distilled, concentrated, exaggerated, enlarged, making (if he chose) a small shadow grow enormous and a little window glitter like a great jewel. He, like two other great poet-dramatists, Aeschylus and (in *Rosmersholm* especially) Ibsen, compressed the anxieties of his time into the plot and image of a curse. Today I wish to say something of those anxieties in more concrete terms, mention what followed, and comment a little on the Elizabethan censorship, which made certain direct utterances impossible.

During the last decade of the reign evidence abounds of uncertainty and unrest. The Armada had shown that Spain could be defeated, but not that she would not return; the worst of several Spanish scares occurred in 1599, after Philip II had died. Across the Channel thirty years of civil war had ended, and the old enemy, so conveniently rent during most of the Queen's reign, had now found in Henry of Navarre as bright and dangerous a star as Henry V had ever been of England. Even the Dutch were beginning to emerge as a potential threat.

At home many who had come to believe in the centralized authority established by the Tudors almost as a law of nature were beginning to fear its total breakdown. In 1593 Peter Wentworth dared once again to demand in Parliament that the Queen entail the succession, and was sent to the Tower, where he died; even prudent Francis Bacon questioned the royal prerogative. Towards the end, in the famous debate on monopolies, Elizabeth had most of the House of Commons against her and made a spectacular virtue of the necessity to yield. The Anglican Establishment grew ever more authoritarian, as it sensed or imagined increasing perils from, on the right, the Catholic infiltration financed from Rome and Spain, and, on the left, the many groups loosely and inaccurately put together under the name of Puritan. Charges of atheism, few of them justifiable, became more and more common as men asked themselves, in the words of Giordano Bruno—Bruno, who had dedicated two works to Sir Philip Sidney—'Why turn to vain fancies when there is experience to teach us?' The commercial classes looked with envy beyond Tudor paternalism to the commercial liberalism of the Dutch, and hour after restless hour, day after rapacious day, a society ever more acquisitive as the opportunities enlarged thrust ceaselessly at the ancient dykes of order and degree.

This general ferment, of which the most vivid expression at the end of the reign was Essex's rebellion, found release in many popular sayings and ballads: ''Twas never merry world since gentlemen came up'; 'The golden world is past and gone.' Pasquil, envisaging the Queen's death, and professing to speak the mind 'of many thousands in this land', remarked, 'He shall do me a pleasure that cuts my throat.' Bacon recalled a popular prophecy,

> When HEMPE is spun,
> England's done,

(HEMPE being the initials of the Tudor sovereigns, Henry, Edward, Mary, Philip, Elizabeth.) We learn John of Gaunt's speech at school, but usually break off after the cascade of substantives and epithets:

> This land of such dear souls, this dear, dear land,
> Dear for her reputation through the world,

and before the principle verb,

> Is now leas'd out, I die pronouncing it,
> Like to a tenement or pelting farm.

All in all, that Tudor dynasty for whom its founder, at the close of *Richard III*, prayed with such a fervour of hope, was ending in uncertainty at the time that speech was written.

There is no space here, but attention might, I think, again be given to the Elizabethan censorship in those final years. Nashe, Jonson, Kyd, Deloney, Marlowe, Sir John Hayward, the anonymous writer of *Sir Thomas Moore* (in part perhaps Shakespeare's own), were all in trouble, most of it political trouble, and we know that the deposition scene in *Richard II* was removed from the First and Second Quartos. To put oneself in the same camp as Dr. Rowse may be unwise, and Mr. Crow, with whom it is dangerous to disagree, has warned me that people in the 1590s could not possibly have used the word 'art' in connection with playwriting; yet, when Shakespeare listed among the wrongs that led him to contemplate suicide, 'Art, made tongue-tied by authority',

I cannot help suspecting some trouble with the censor. He may not indeed have wished to write onward from Richard III into closer contemporary history, but it is certain that, had he sought to express the fears and conflicts nearer his own time directly, he would have been forbidden. Knowledge that work a writer desires to do will be done without hope of seeing the light often affects the work he does instead; and it is also certain that, as the century was turning, so Shakespeare himself turned to the eternal human weaknesses which nourish the fears and conflicts of all ages and are nourished by them. Behind him lay the histories and the radiant comedies, ahead lay the tragedies; and, as it were, in the gateway, stands one character who partakes of all.

This is Malvolio. In all the plays there is not, to my mind, a grimmer or more shiveringly prophetic line than his final curtain, 'I'll be revenged on the whole pack of you!' And half a century later, what a revenge it was! The gay self-indulgent Orsinos and Olivias, the Sir Tobys, Sir Andrews and Marias had been routed, the Puritans were triumphant and the theatres closed. England had again succumbed to the civil war against which all the bells in all the history plays had been rung to warn her.

I don't of course mean that Shakespeare intended Malvolio as a portrait of a Puritan, as Ben Jonson intended Zeal-of-the-Land Busy. Maria, having called him one, almost immediately takes it back. But this one line of hers, and all that is attributed to him, would have been enough for the audience to take him for one. Whether or not the Puritans were really spoil-sports in the Victorian sense, 'obsessed with sex and opposed to fun', as Mr. Christopher Hill says they were not, they were so to the groundlings, and from Malvolio's first entry they could not have failed to associate him with Puritanism. Years later one of the most lovable of Puritans, Lucy Hutchinson, wrote:

All that crossed the views of the needy courtiers . . . could not endure blasphemous oaths, ribald conversation, profane scoffs . . . all these were Puritans: such false logic did the children of darkness use to argue with against the hated children of light, whom they branded beside as illiterate, morose, melancholy, discontented, crazed sort of men . . . as such they were made the sport . . . of every stage, and every table and puppet-play *belched* forth profane scoffs against them, the drunkards made them their songs, and all fiddlers and mimics learned to abuse them.

One feels that she must have witnessed a performance of *Twelfth Night* and written with the indignant memory of Malvolio's ill-treatment still fresh. Moreover, across the title-page of the play in the Second Folio at Windsor, a delicate hand has scored out *Twelfth Night* and written 'Malvolio' in its place. The hand is that of Charles I. It is true that he also crossed out *Henry IV* and wrote 'Falstaff', and *All's Well That Ends Well* and wrote 'Parolles', and may only have been giving to each play the name of the character who stole it. Yet one may suggest that in Malvolio he saw the kind of man who would one day 'be revenged', and in the course of his revenge deprive kingdom of king and king himself of life. It has always seemed to me, although I have never yet seen the play so directed, that Malvolio's exit line should send a cold shudder across the stage. On the one hand, still in their warm Illyrian sunshine, still with leisure to play arpeggios on their exquisite emotions, to be light, entrancing, selfish, irresponsible, with the bells audible for their triple wedding, stand the Duke and Viola, Olivia and Sebastian, Maria and Sir Toby. On the other stands Malvolio, insulted, ridiculed, dishevelled and alone; and as he thunders out his bitter threat, a moment's silence should fall and we should almost hear the muskets. Ahead, in the life of

Shakespeare's imaginings, wait Hamlet, Othello, Macbeth, Lear; ahead, in real life, waits the Civil War, Malvolio's revenge.

August 1966

CONTRIBUTORS

G. P. V. AKRIGG, Professor of English, University of British Columbia.

MURIEL C. BRADBROOK, Professor of English, Mistress of Girton College, University of Cambridge.

JOHN RUSSELL BROWN, Professor and Head of the Department of Drama, University of Birmingham.

MICHAEL BURN, former *Times* correspondent, writer of fiction and social criticism.

ARNOLD EDINBOROUGH, former university lecturer; critic, journalist, editor.

BAMBER GASCOIGNE, former theatre critic for the *Spectator* and *Observer*; writer and critic.

B. W. JACKSON, Professor of English, McMaster University; Director, Stratford Seminars.

L. C. KNIGHTS, Fellow of Queen's College, King Edward VII Professor of English Literature, University of Cambridge.

F. H. MARES, Senior Lecturer in English, University of Melbourne.

JOHN PETTIGREW, Associate Professor of English, McMaster University; Associate Director, Stratford Seminars.

CHARLES TYLER PROUTY, Professor of English, Yale University.

ARTHUR COLBY SPRAGUE, Professor Emeritus, Bryn Mawr College.

HERBERT WHITTAKER, theatre critic, Toronto *Globe and Mail*.

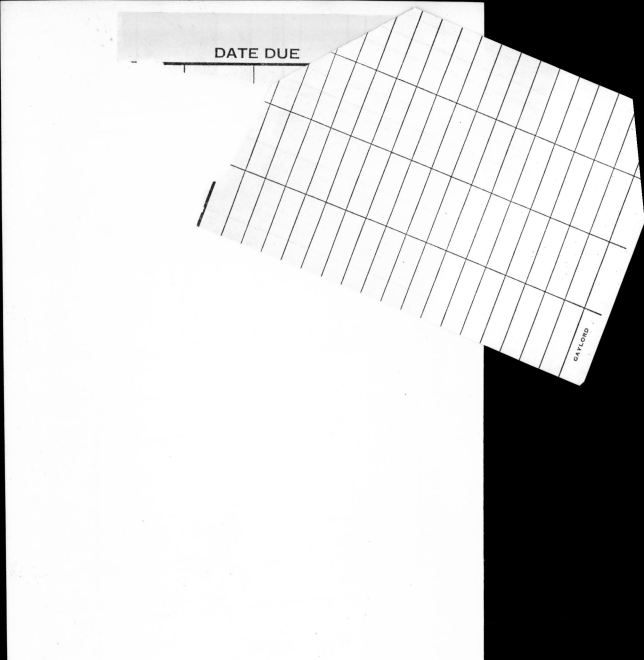

GAYLORD